Positive Quote Coloring for Adults

by BethBirdBooks

Copyright © 2020
All rights reserved.

dreams don't work

unless you do

Your Potential Is *Endless*

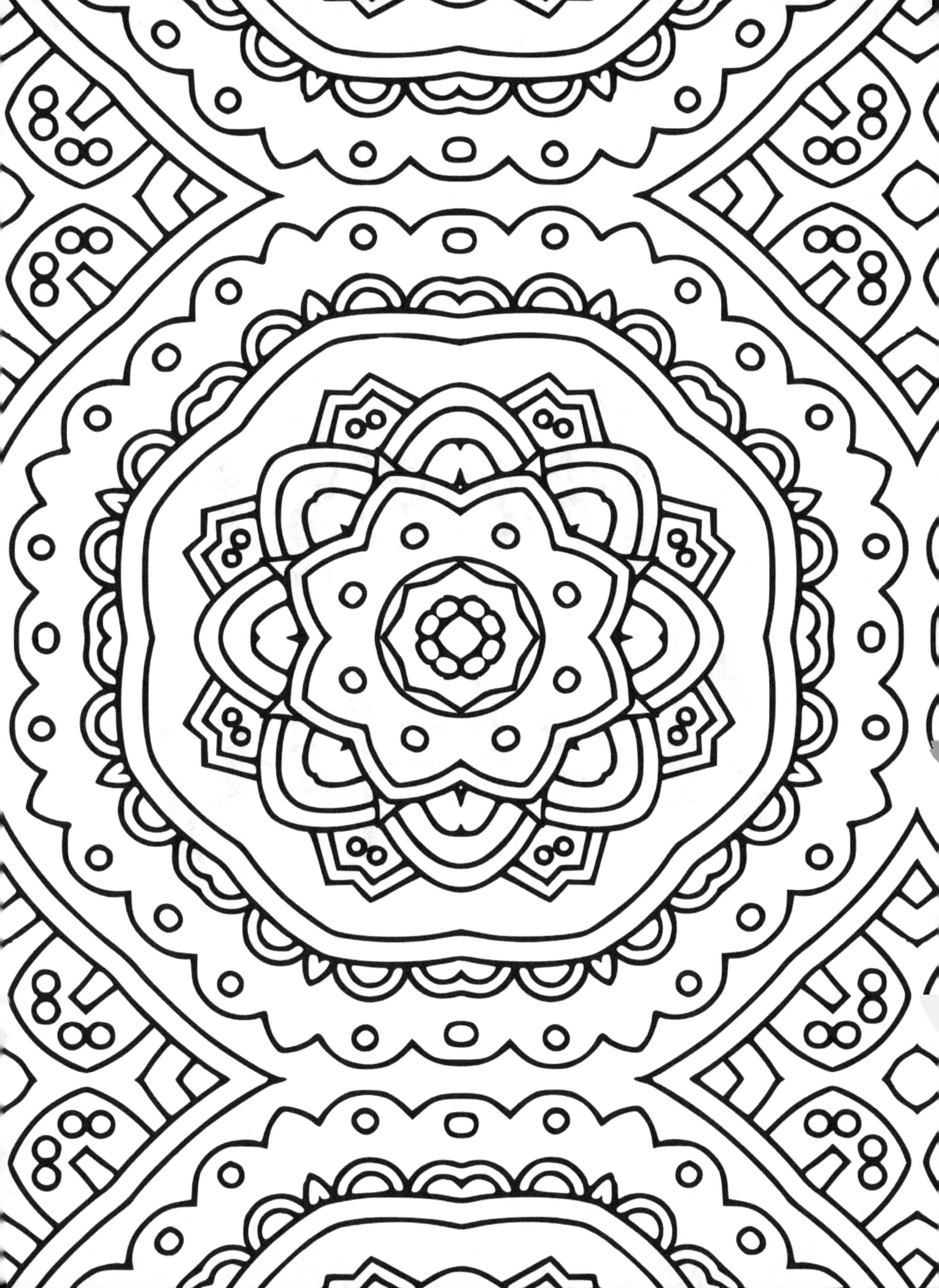

choose happy

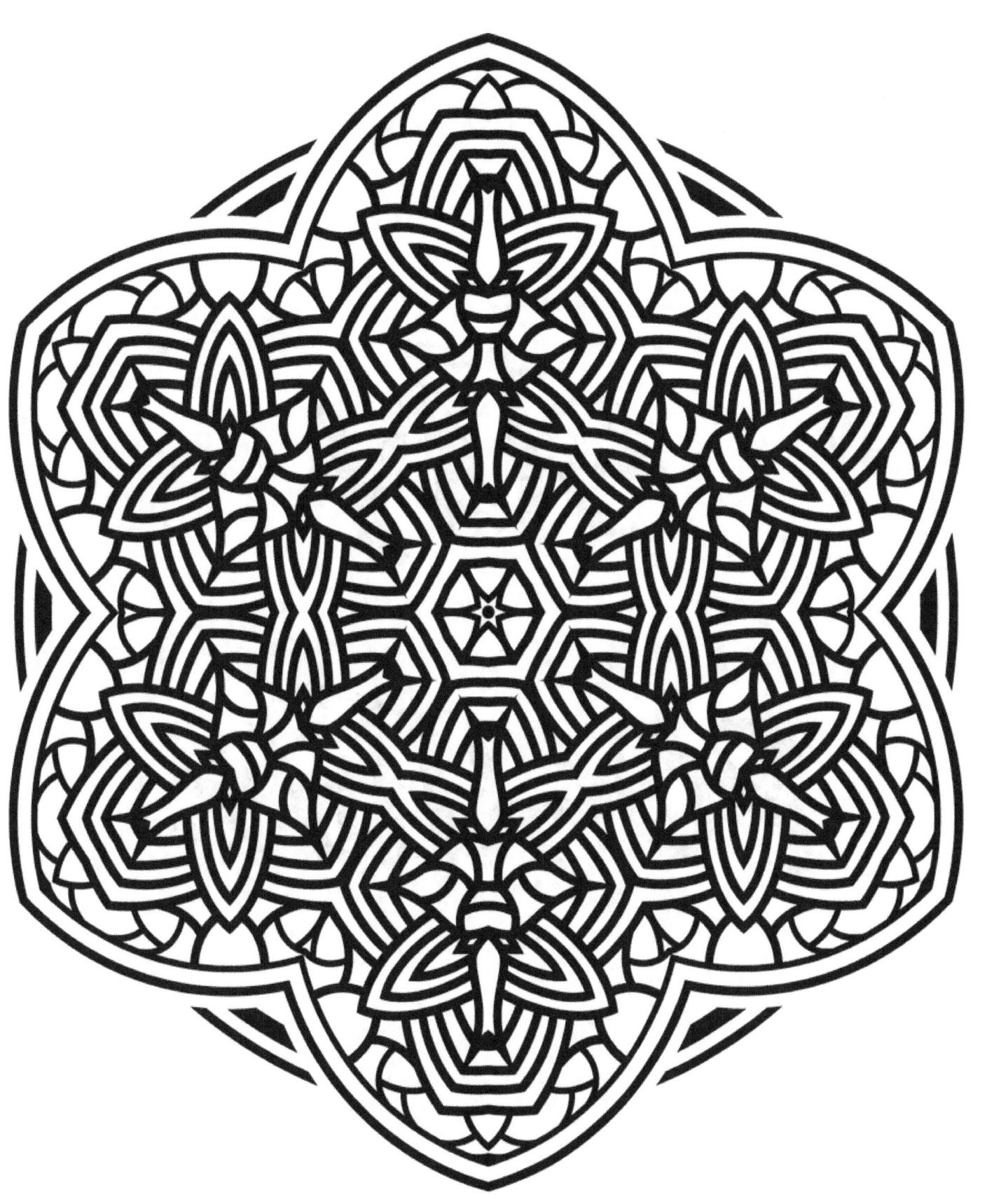

STAY POSITIVE

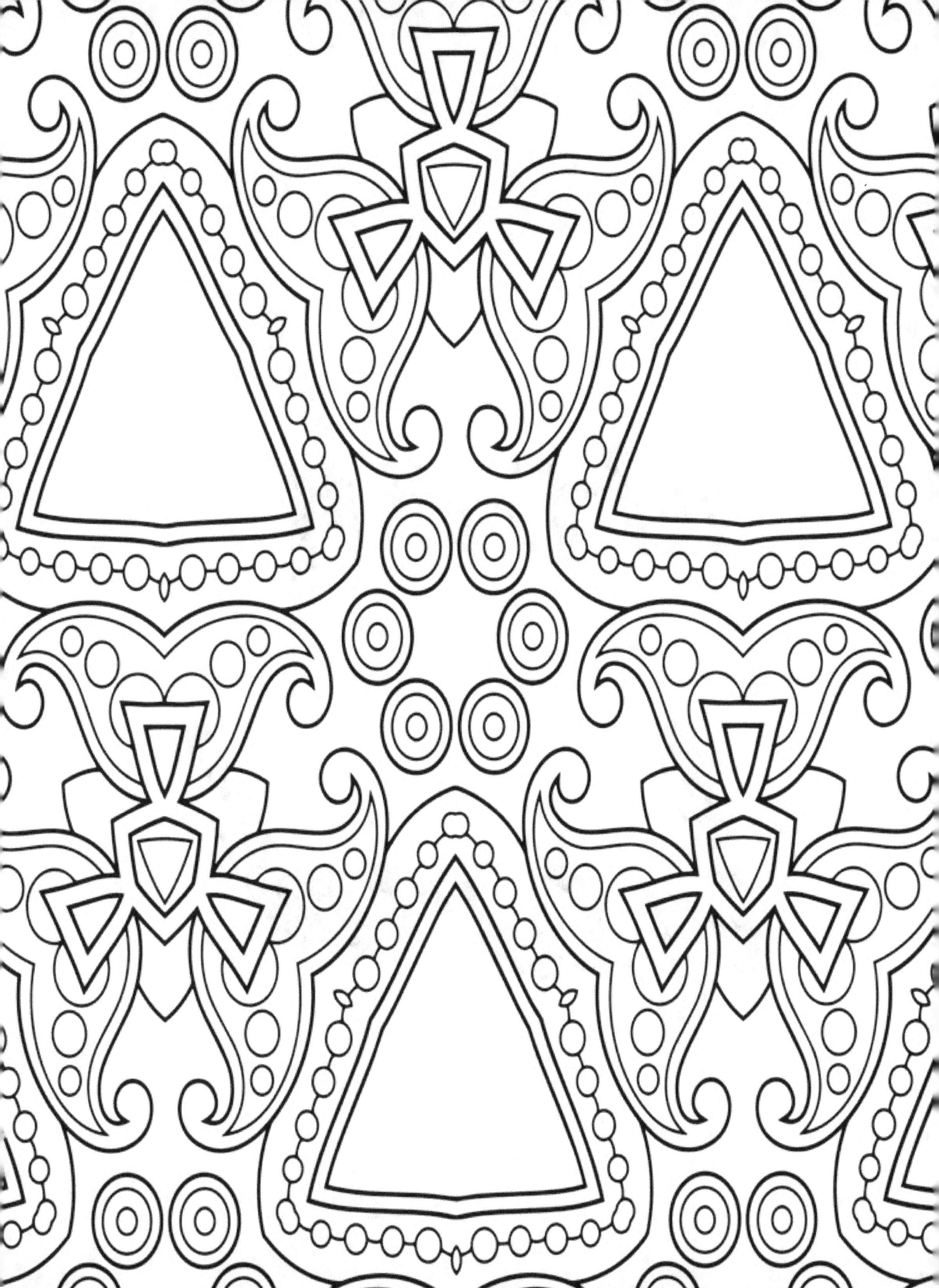

work

hard

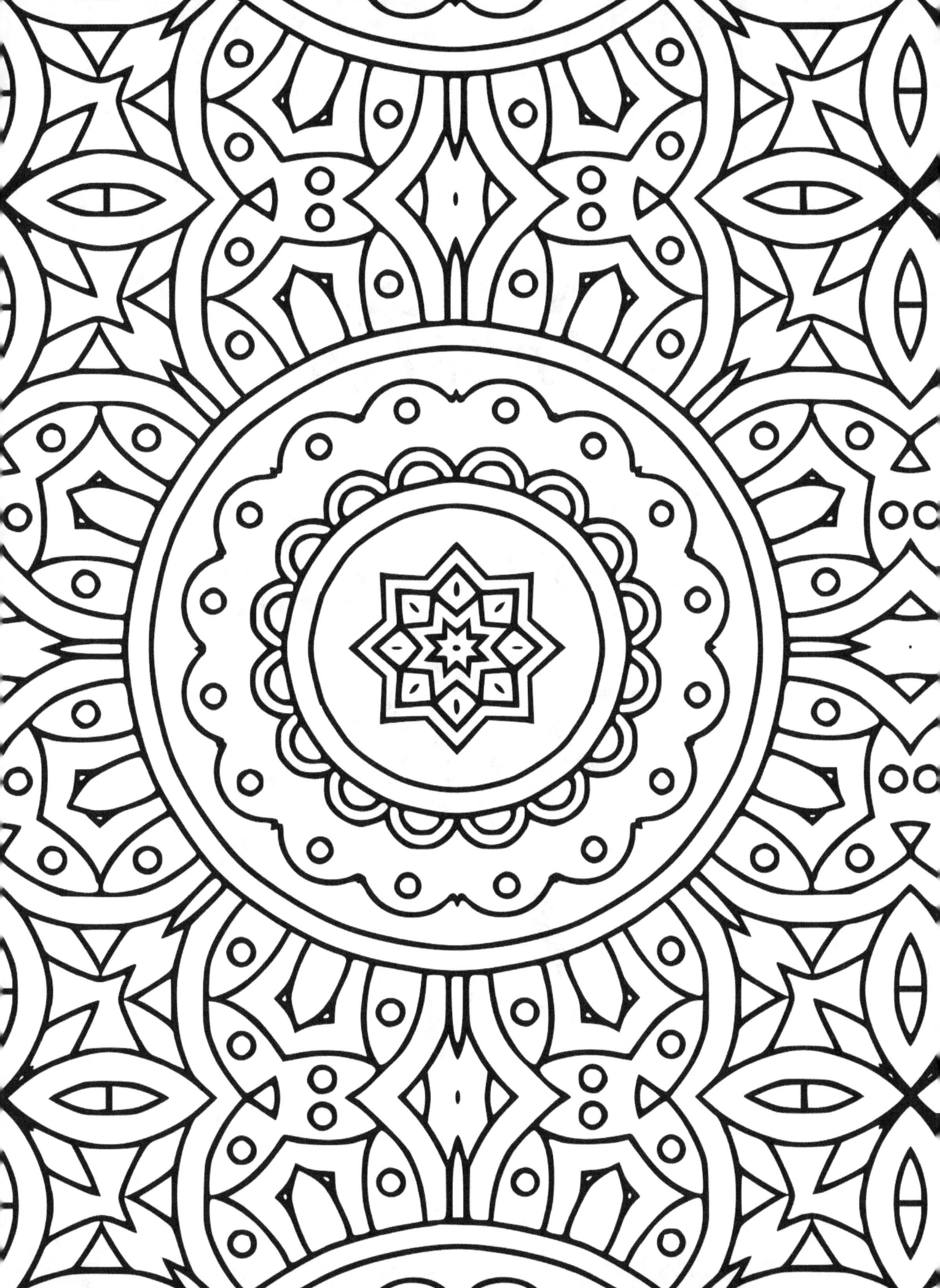

Positive Thoughts Positive Life

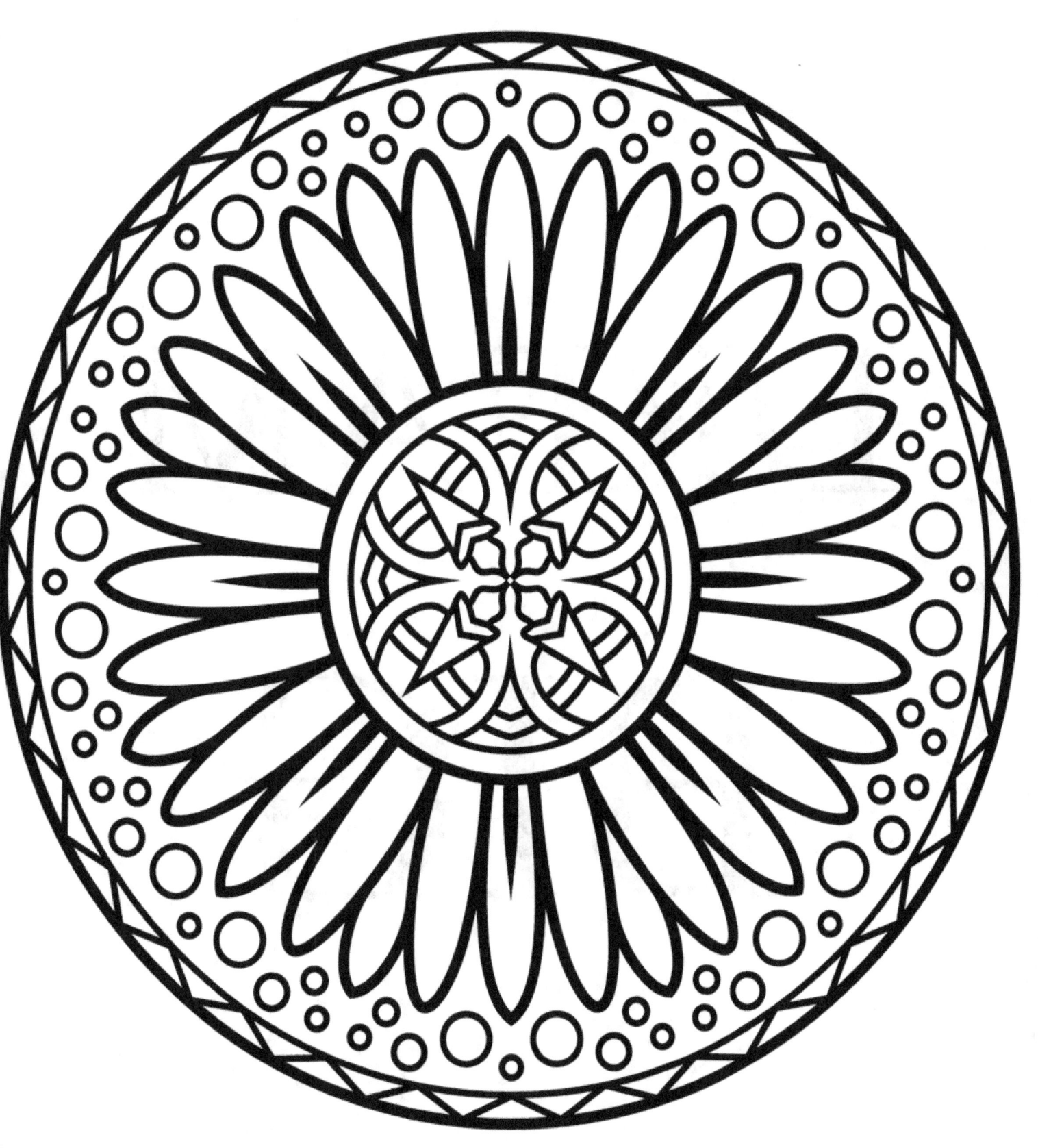

DREAM

BIG

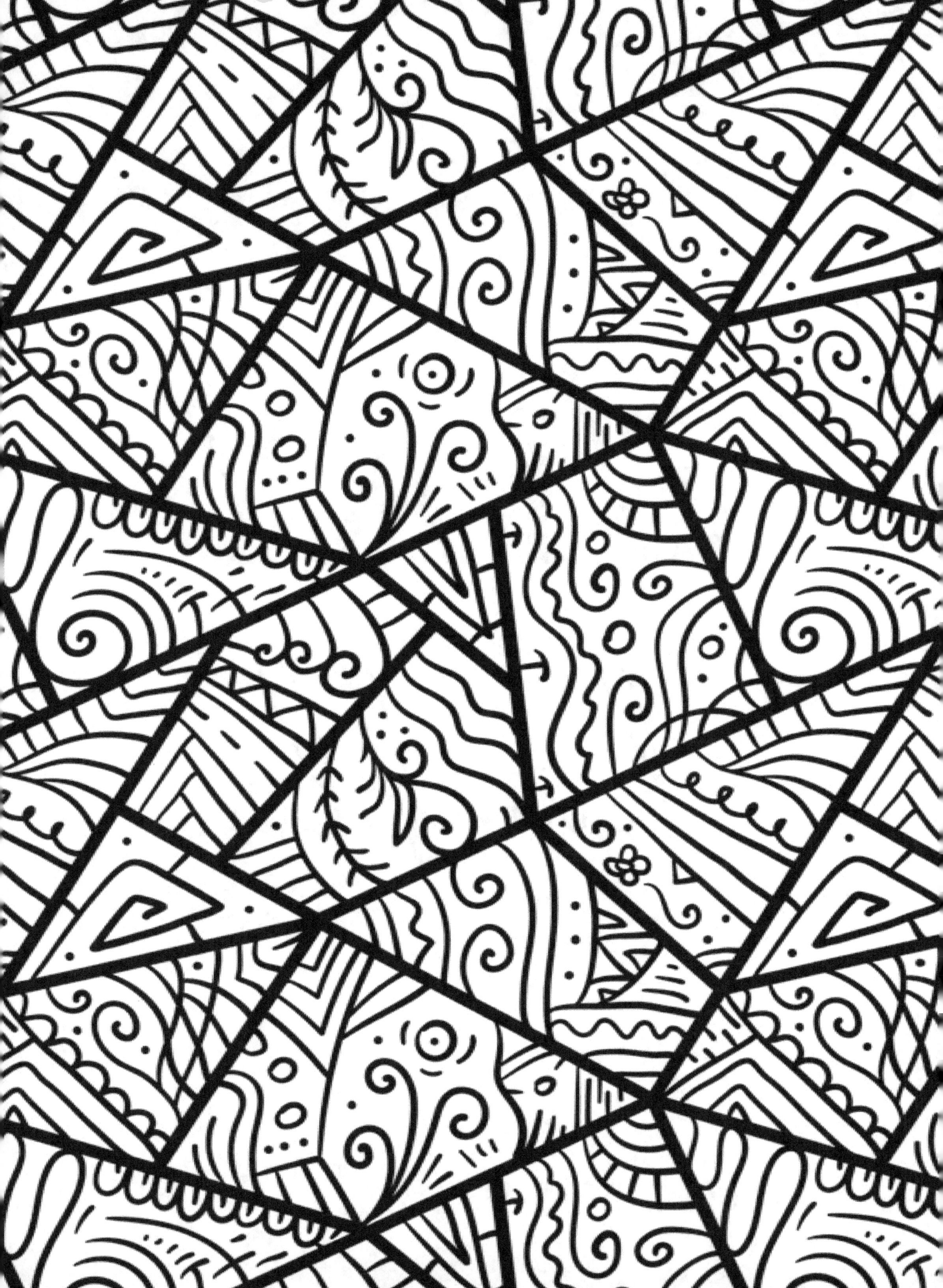

STAY

humble

Smile

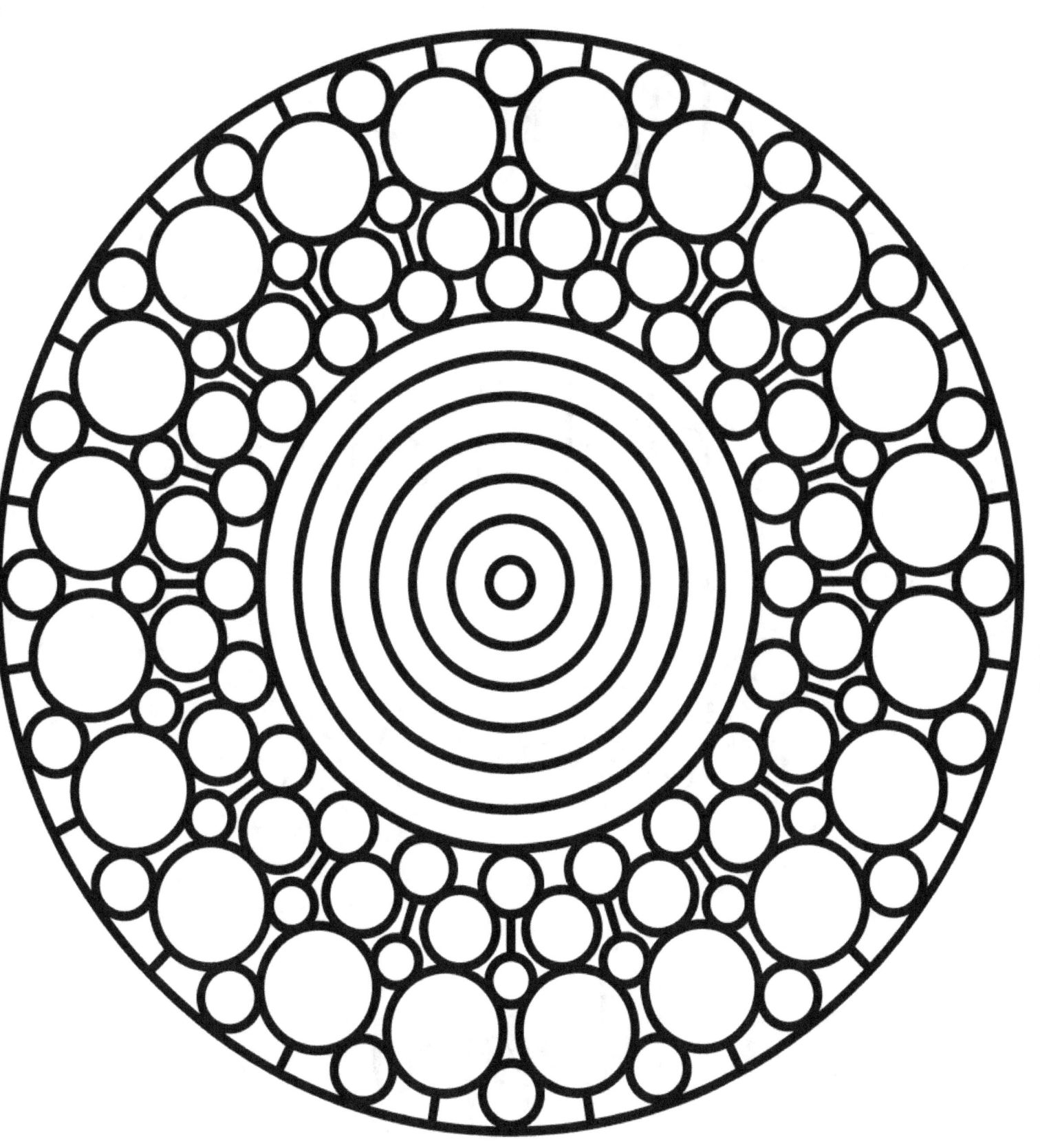

Do More

of What

Makes You

Happy

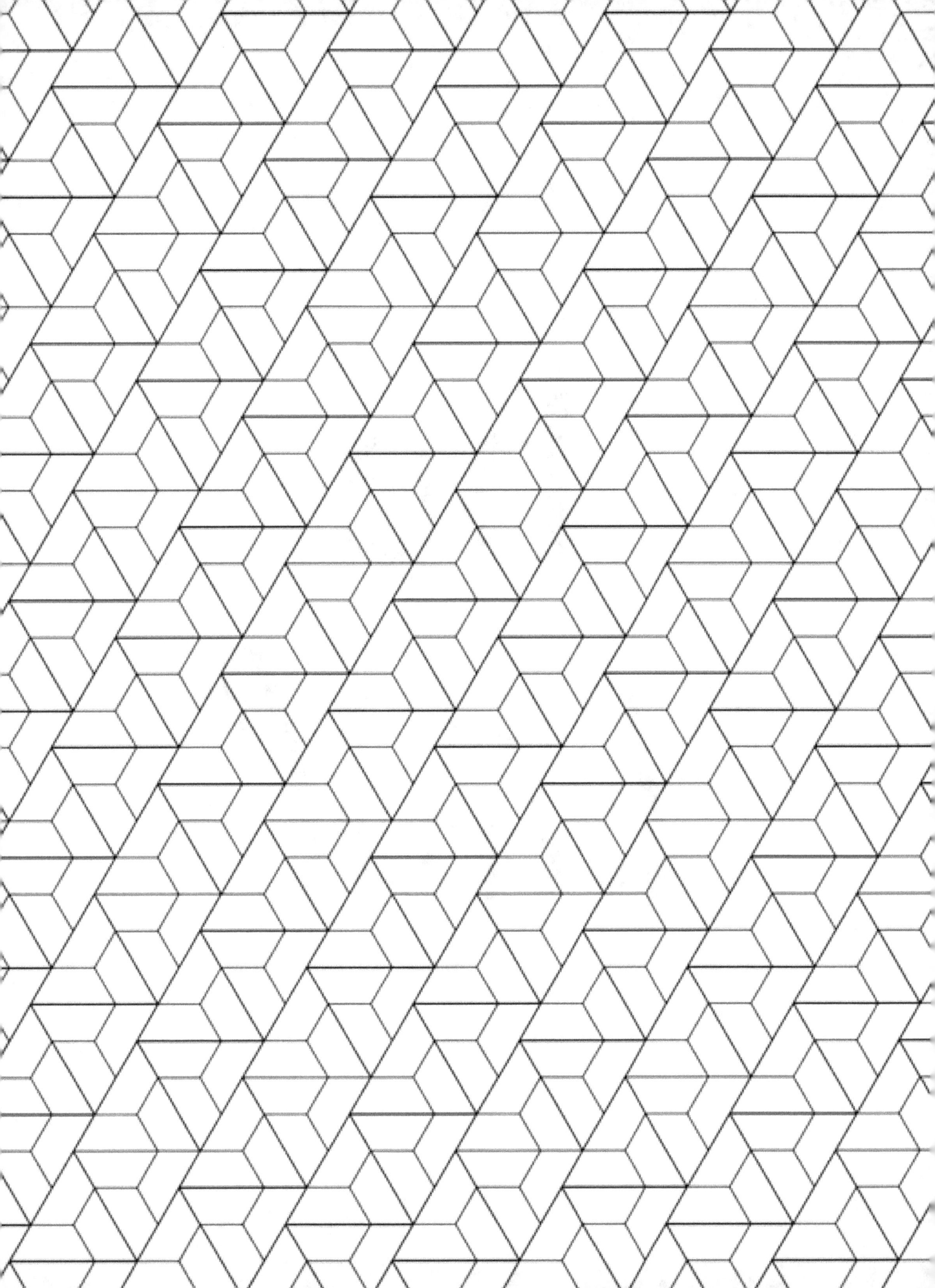

be

kind

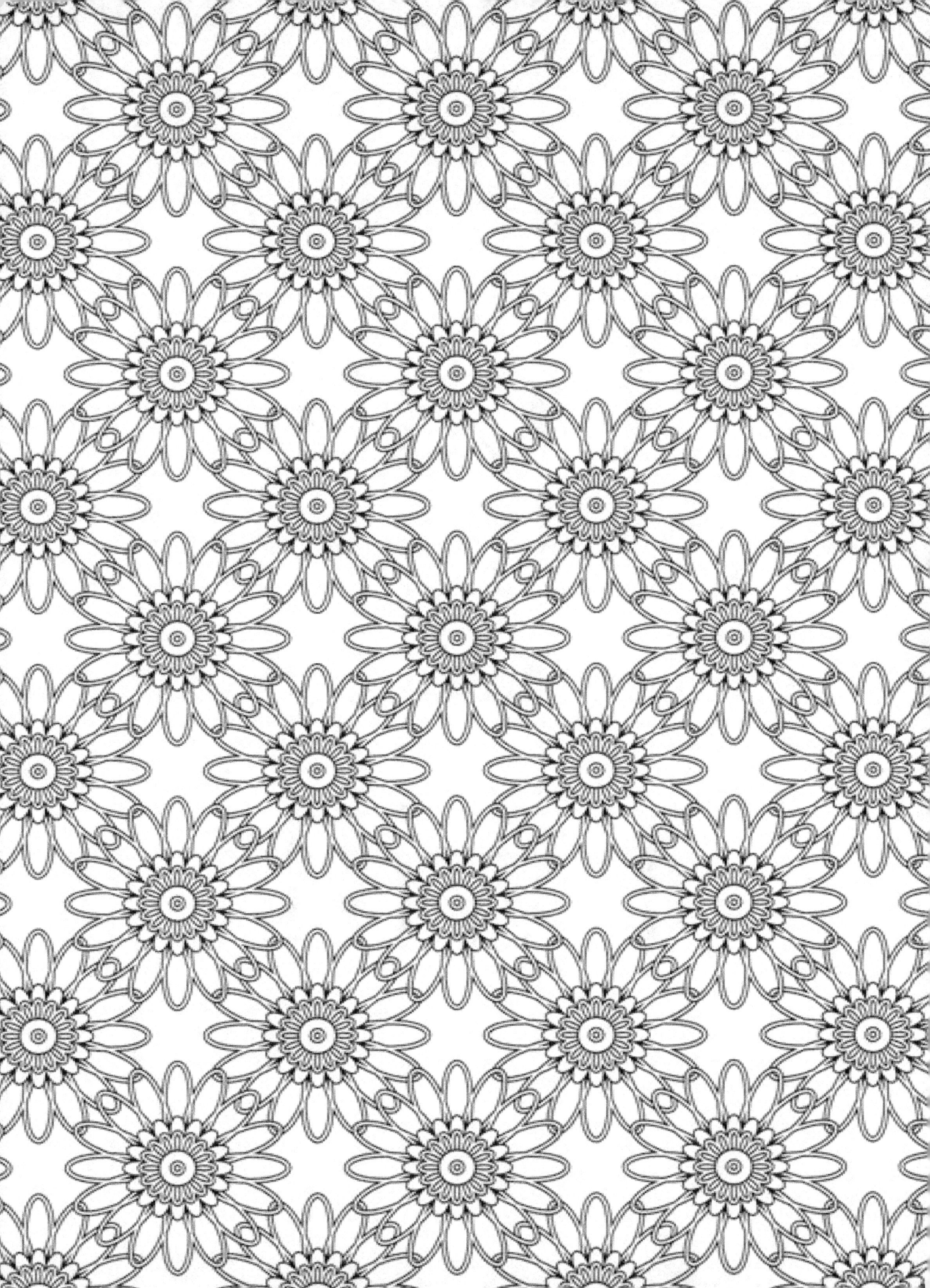

I can

&

I will

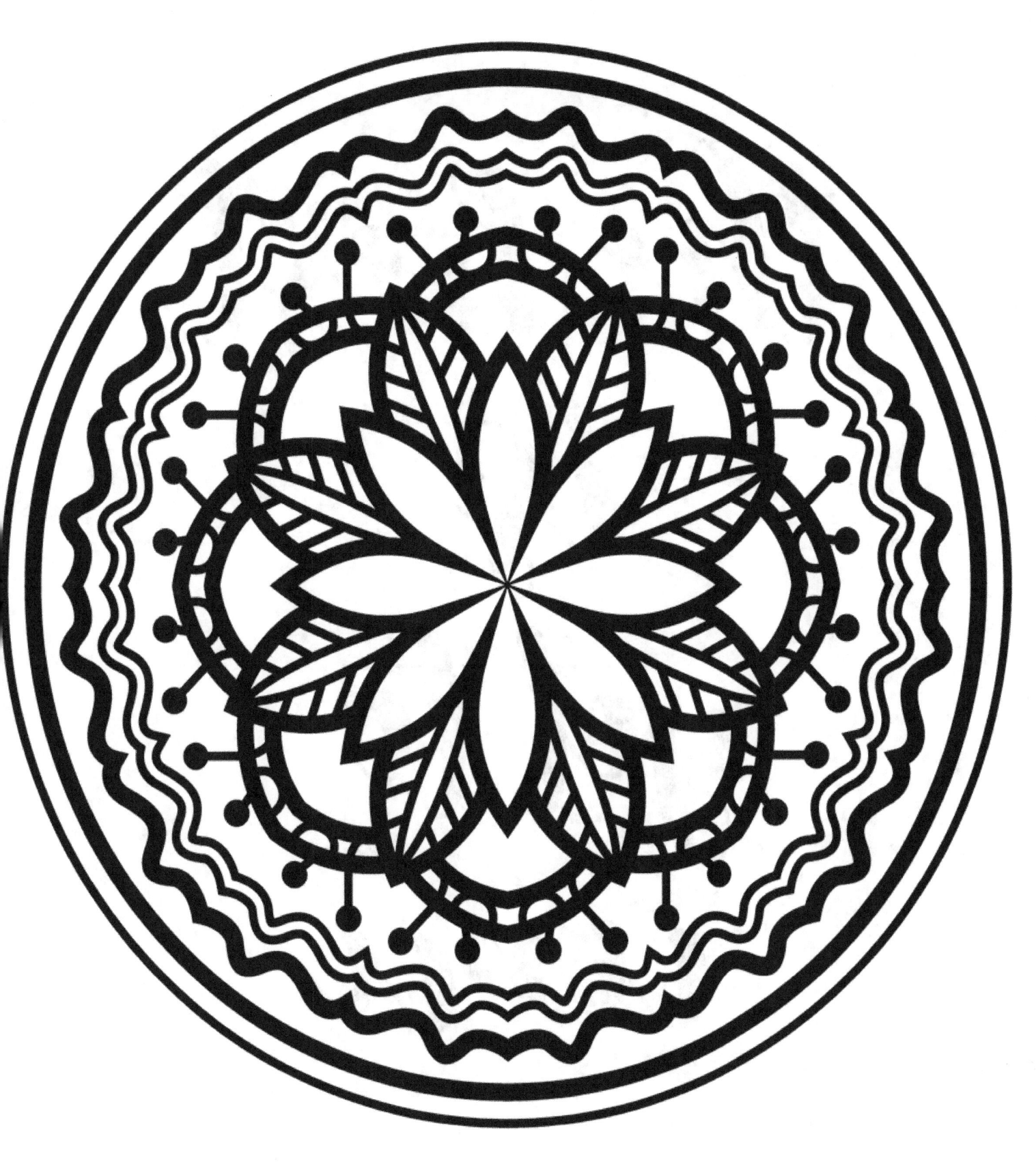

the best is yet to come

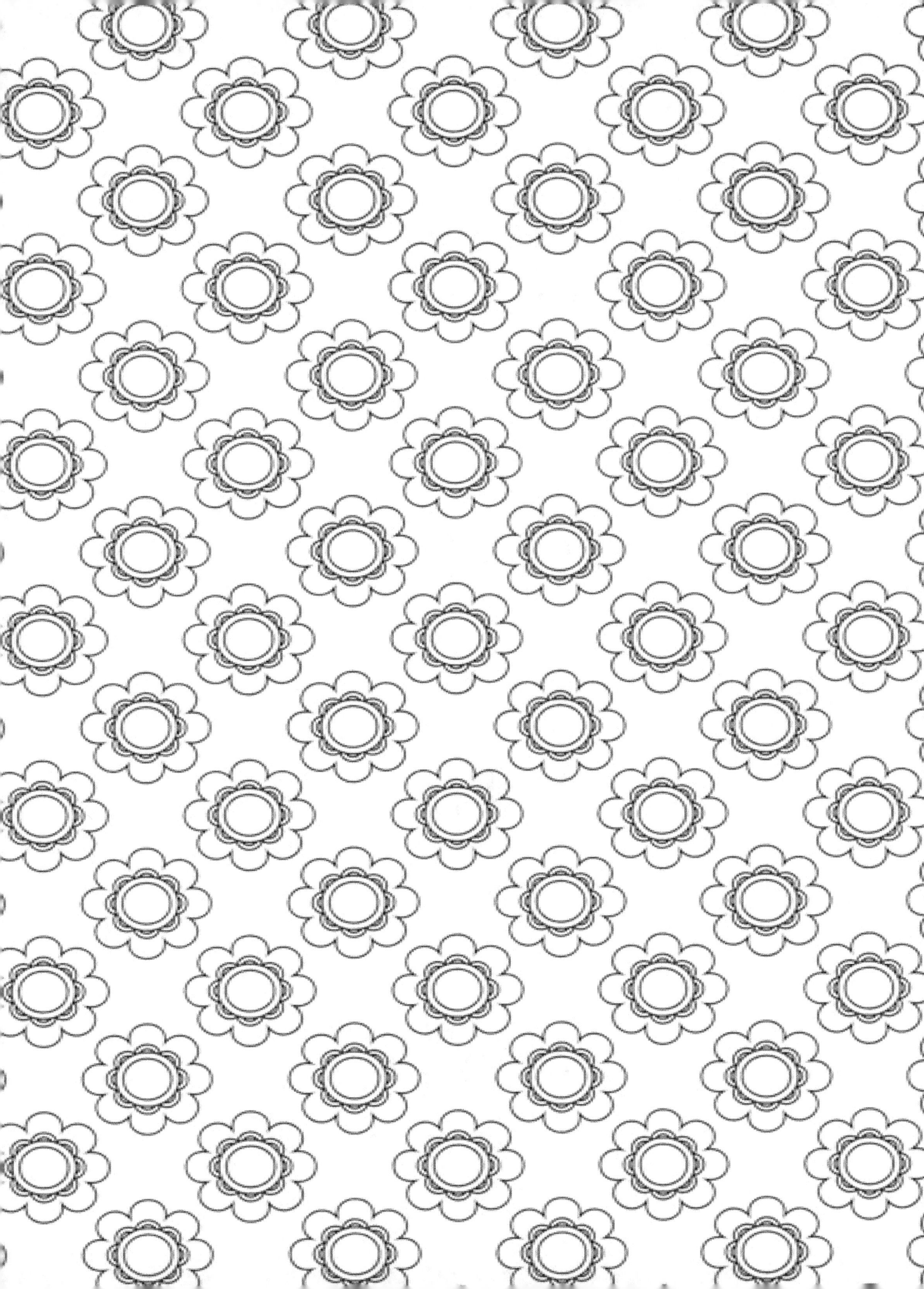

don't

forget

to

smile

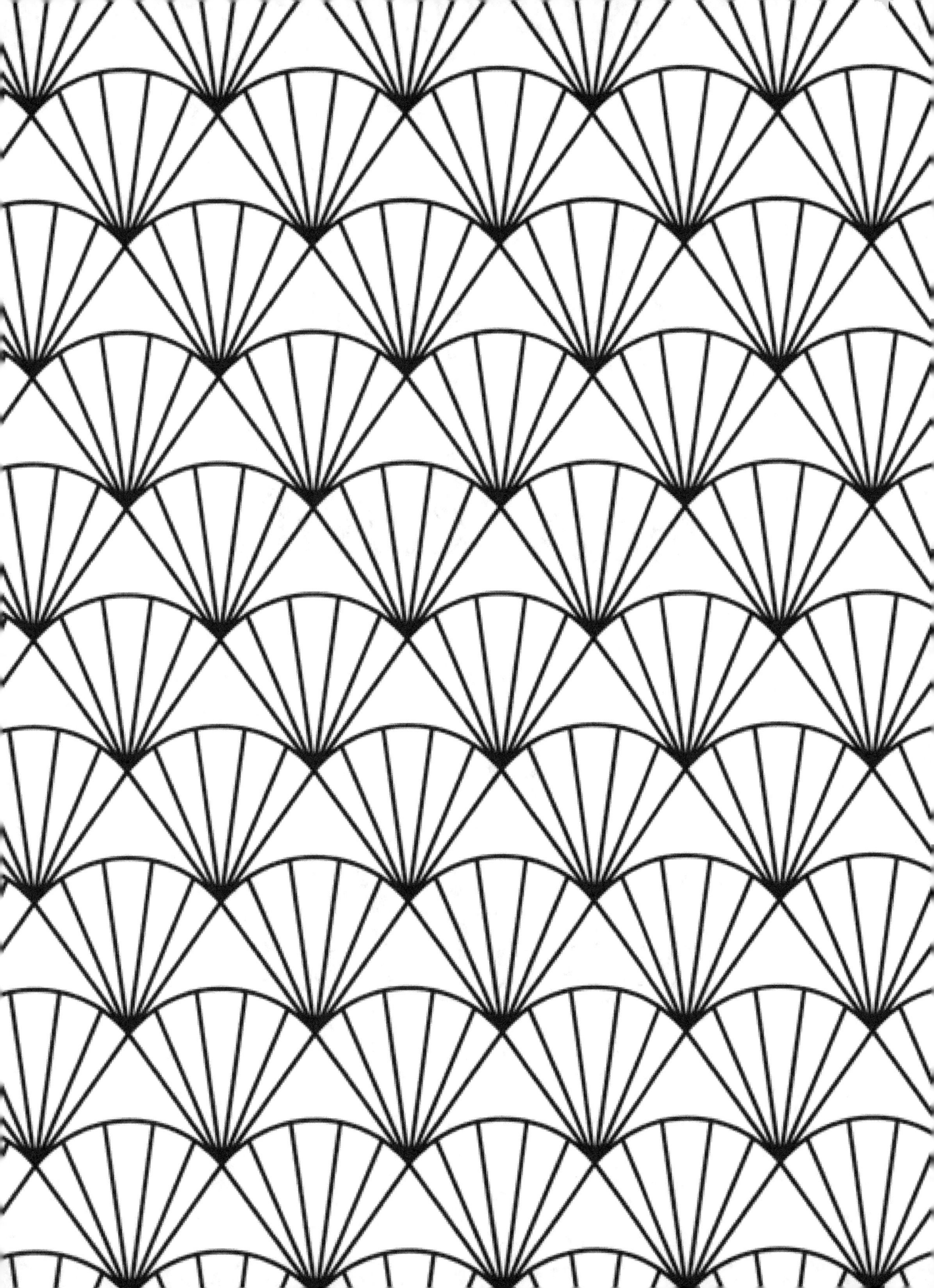

Be your own kind of beautiful

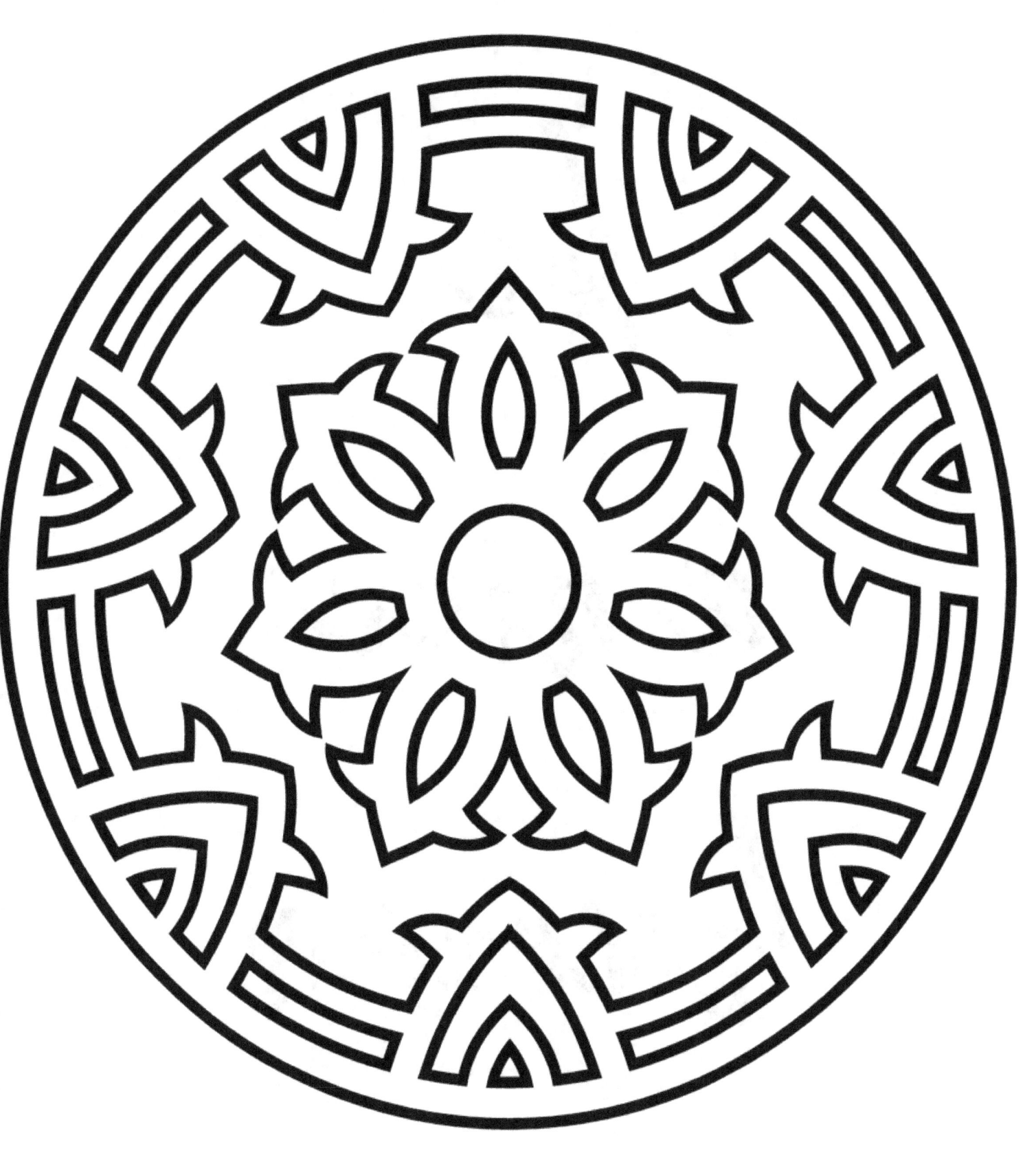

be

a nice

human

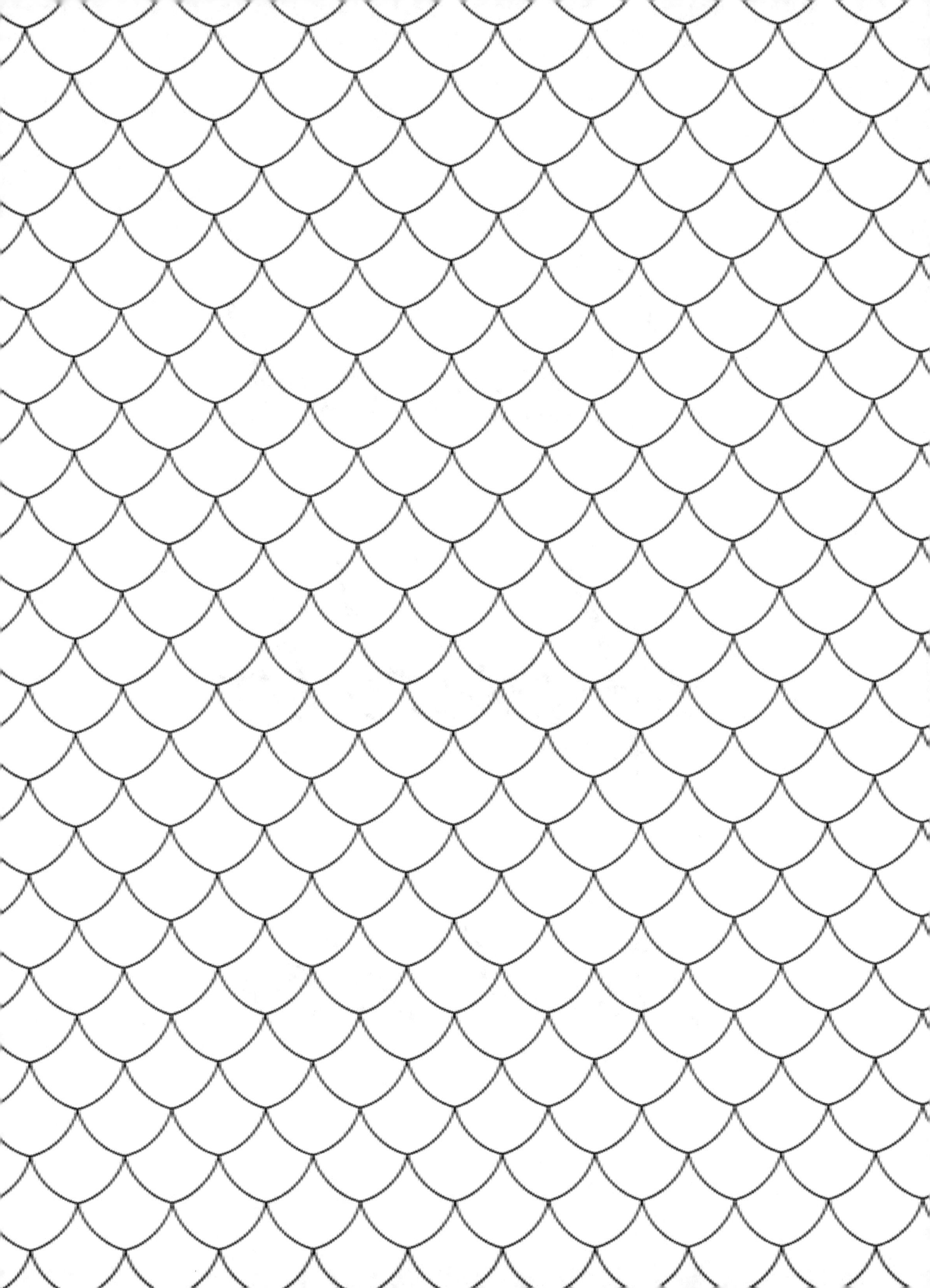

I am not afraid to start over

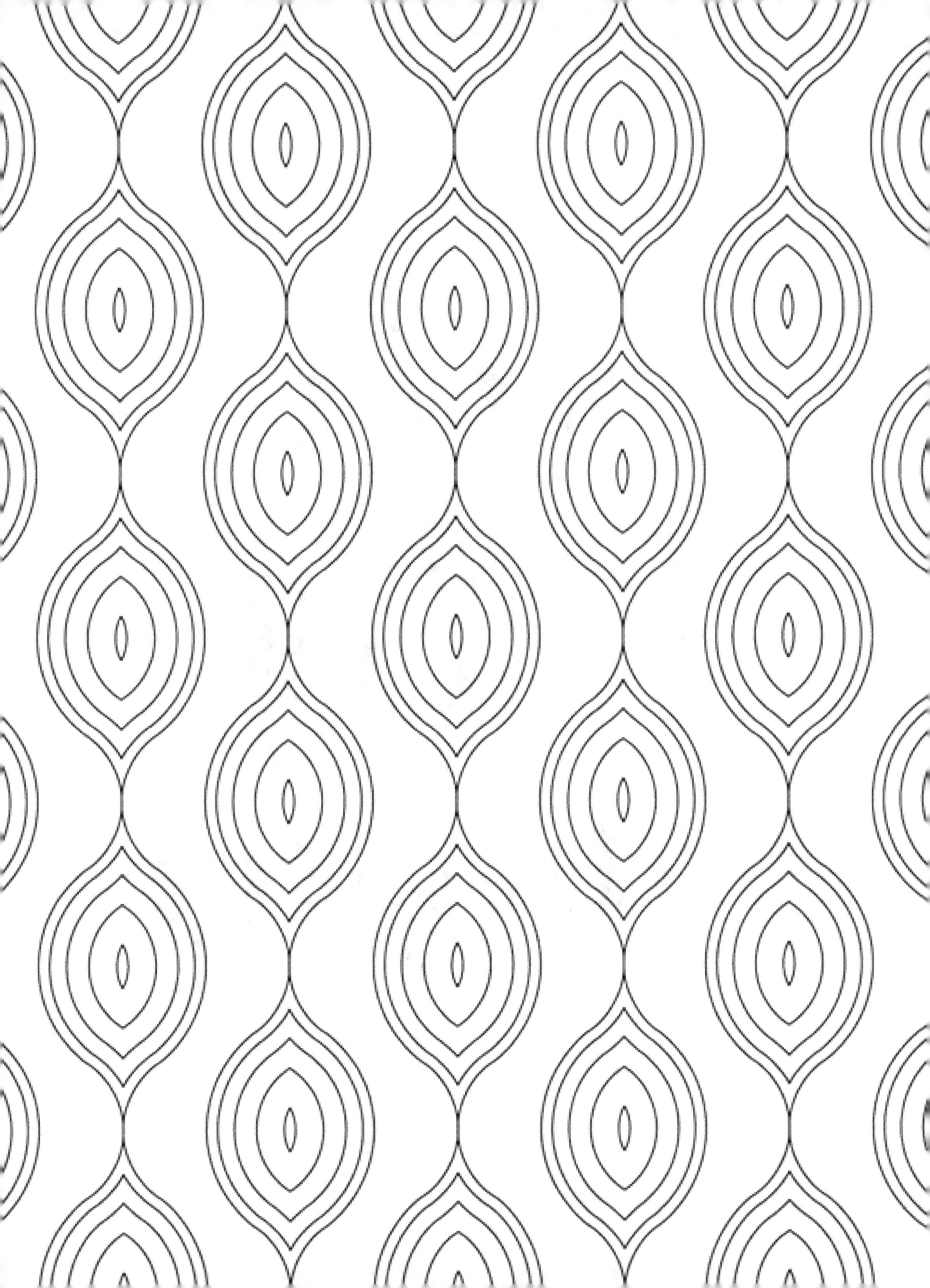

make today amazing

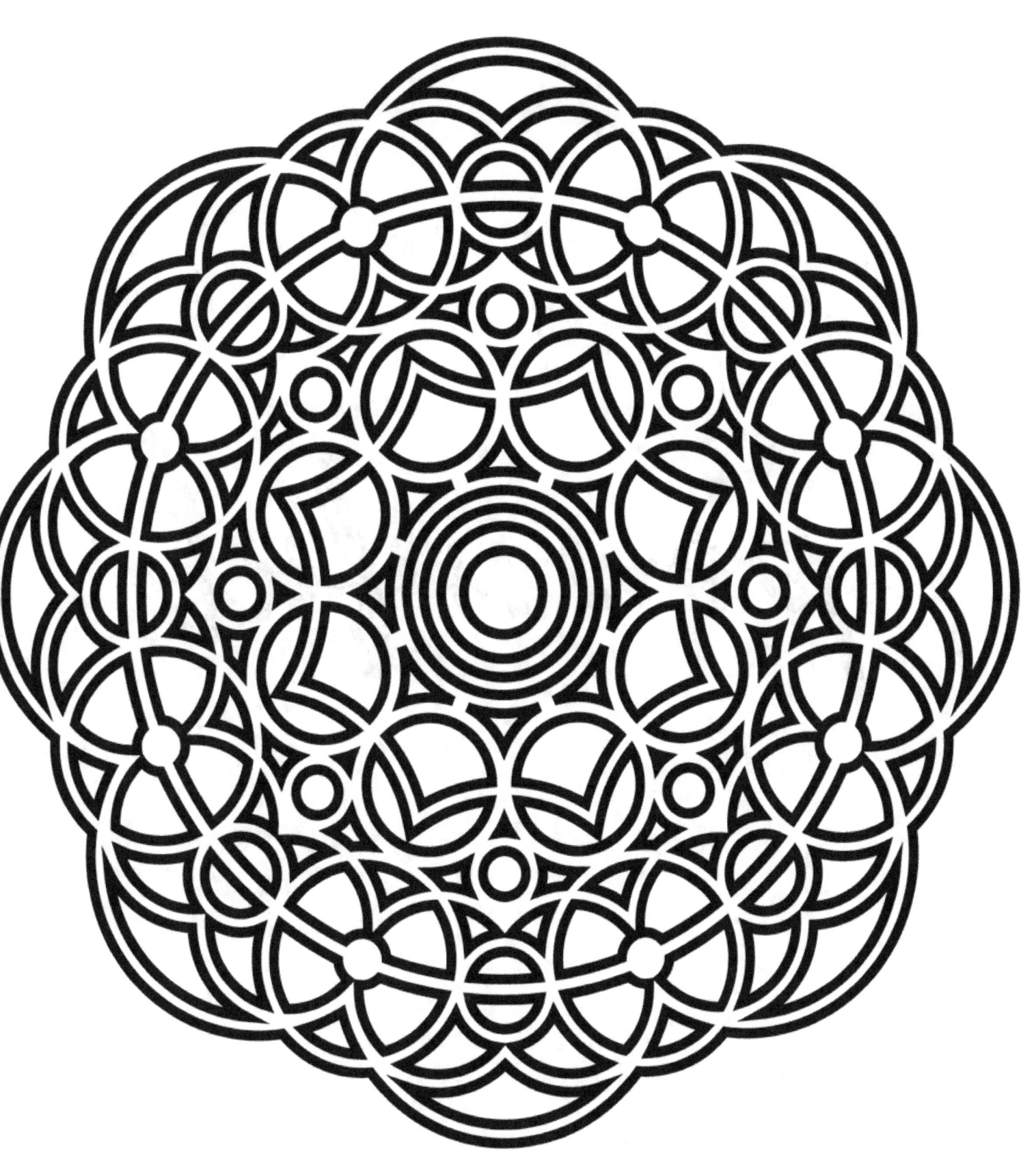

powerful

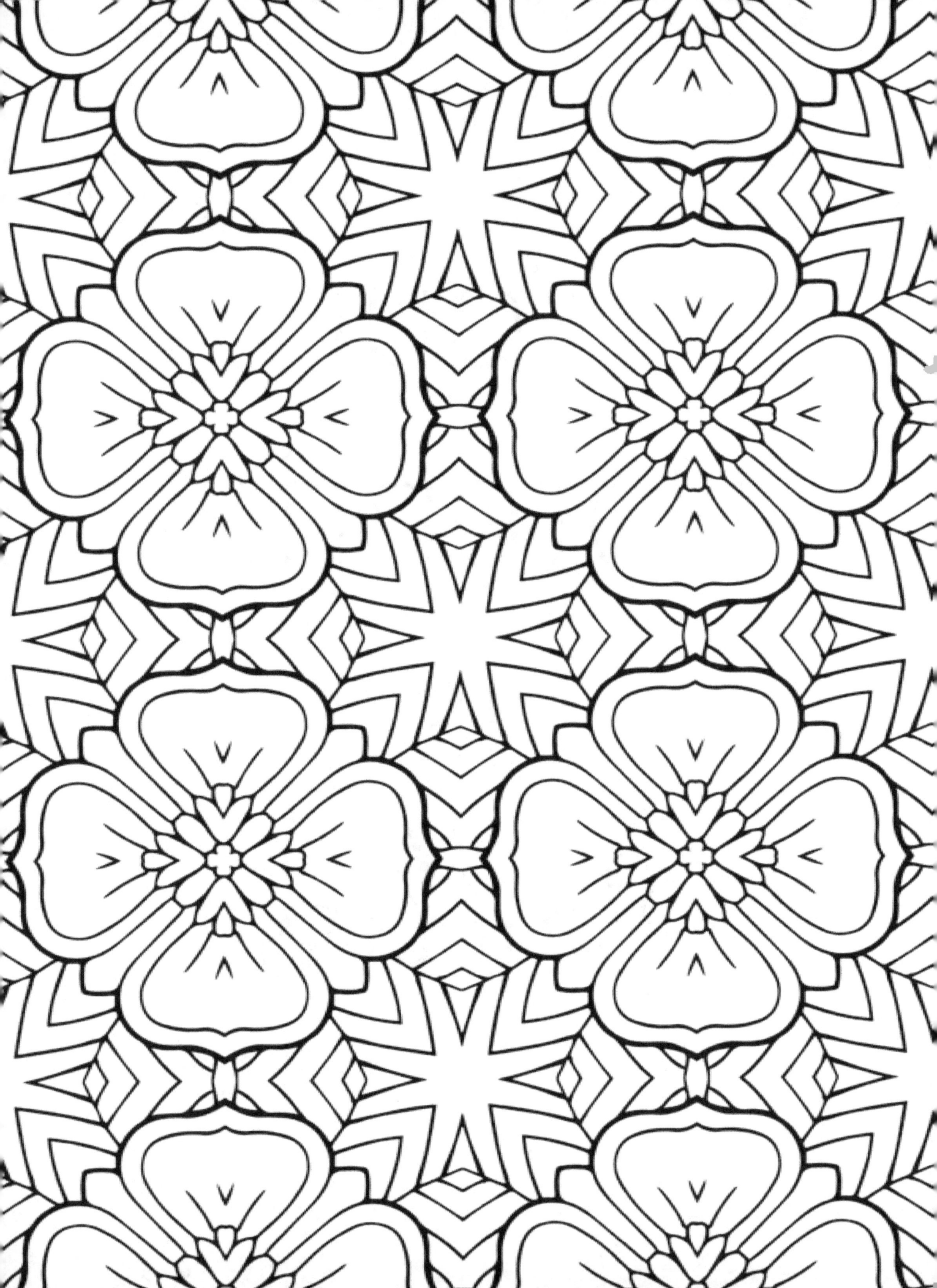

Your Potential Is *Endless*

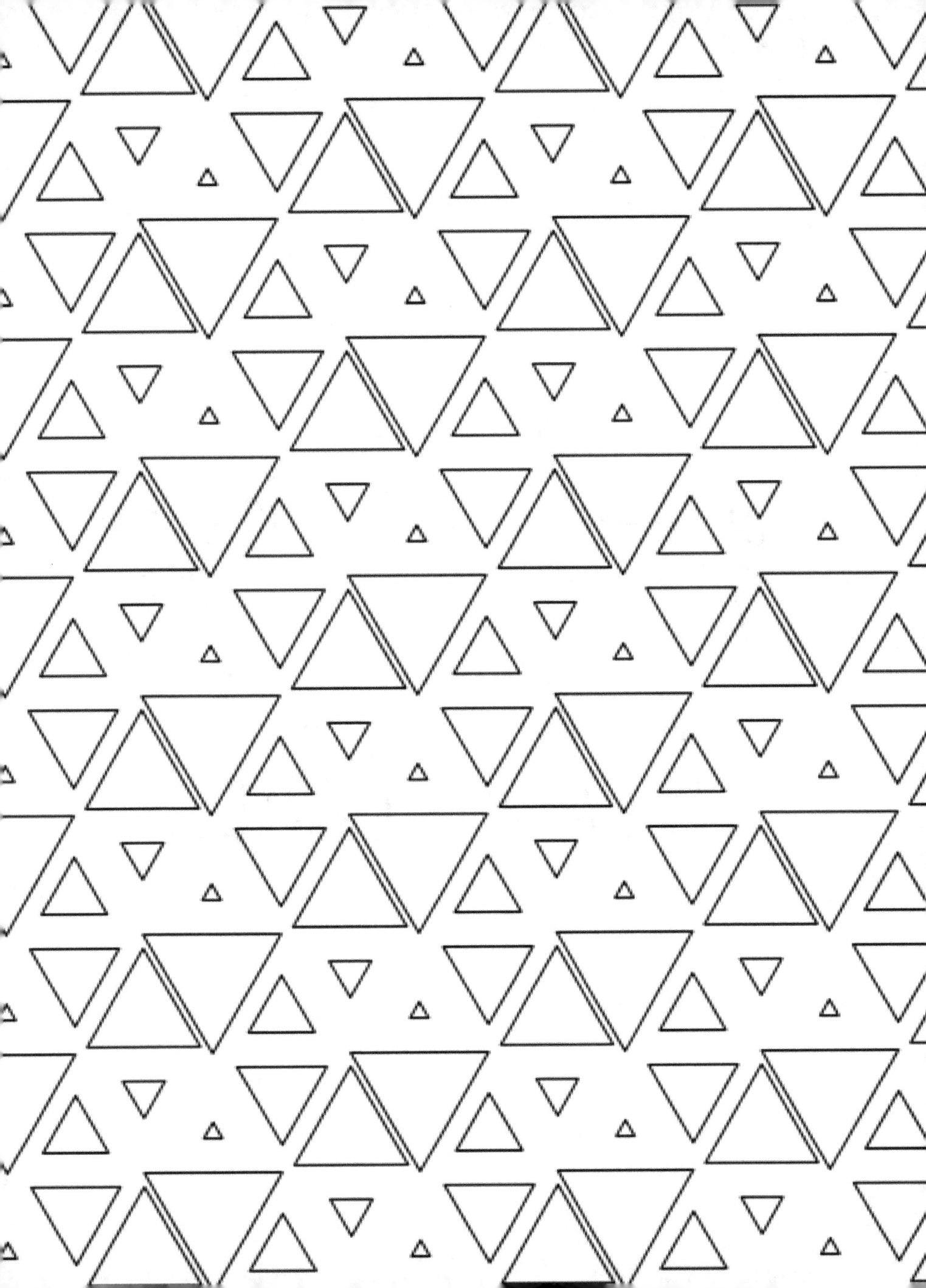

good things take time

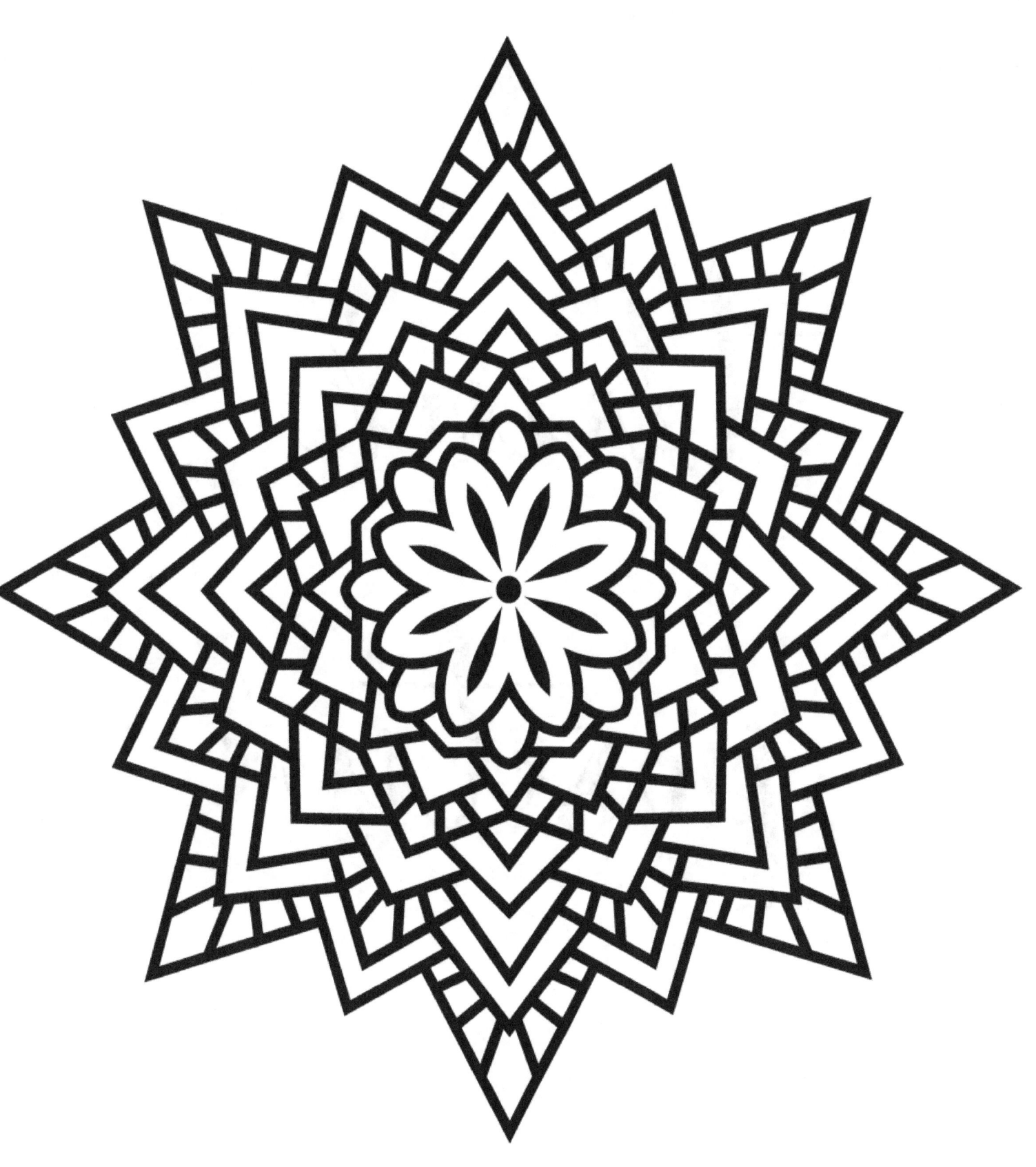

think

positive

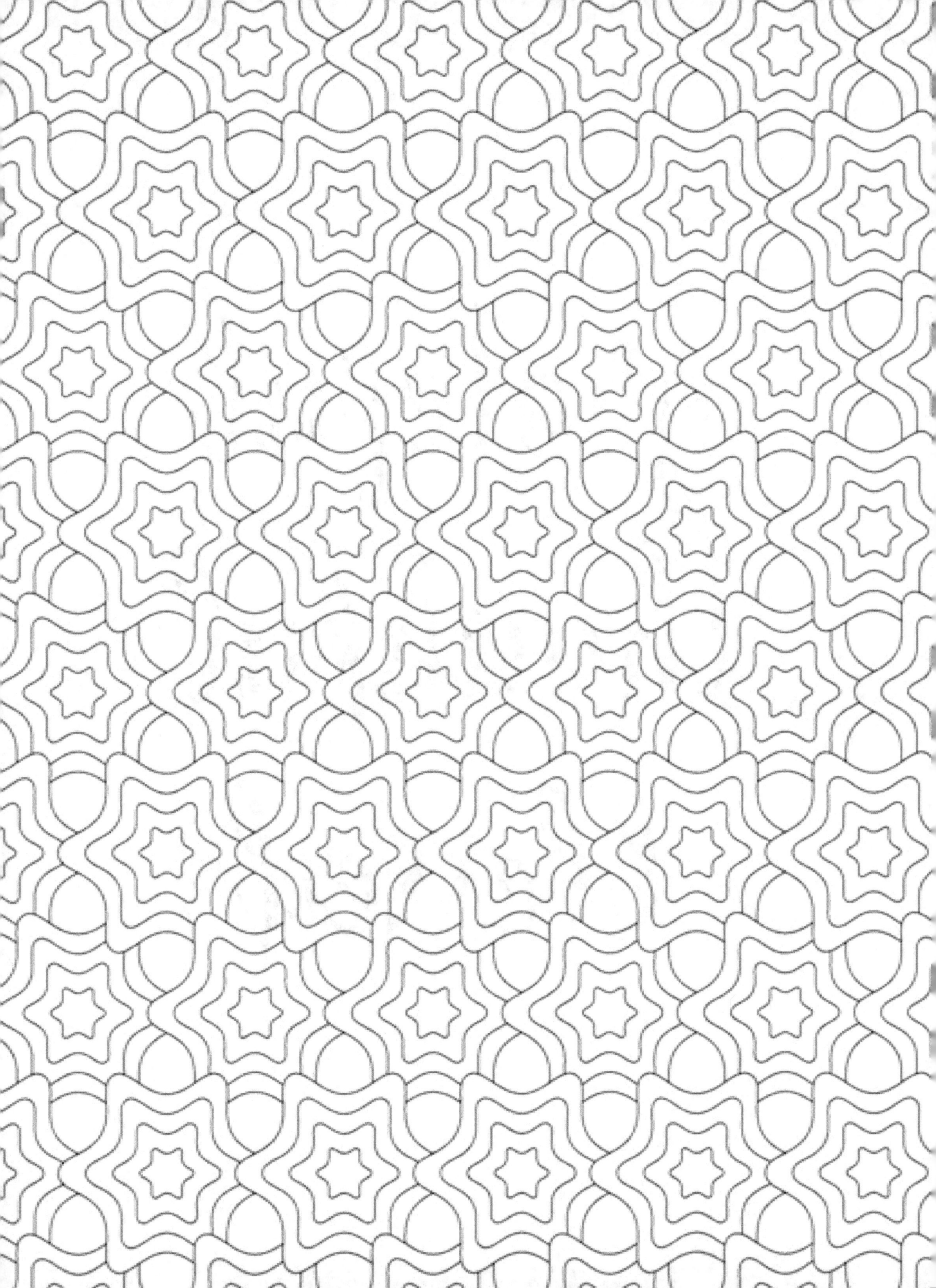

grateful

thankful

blessed

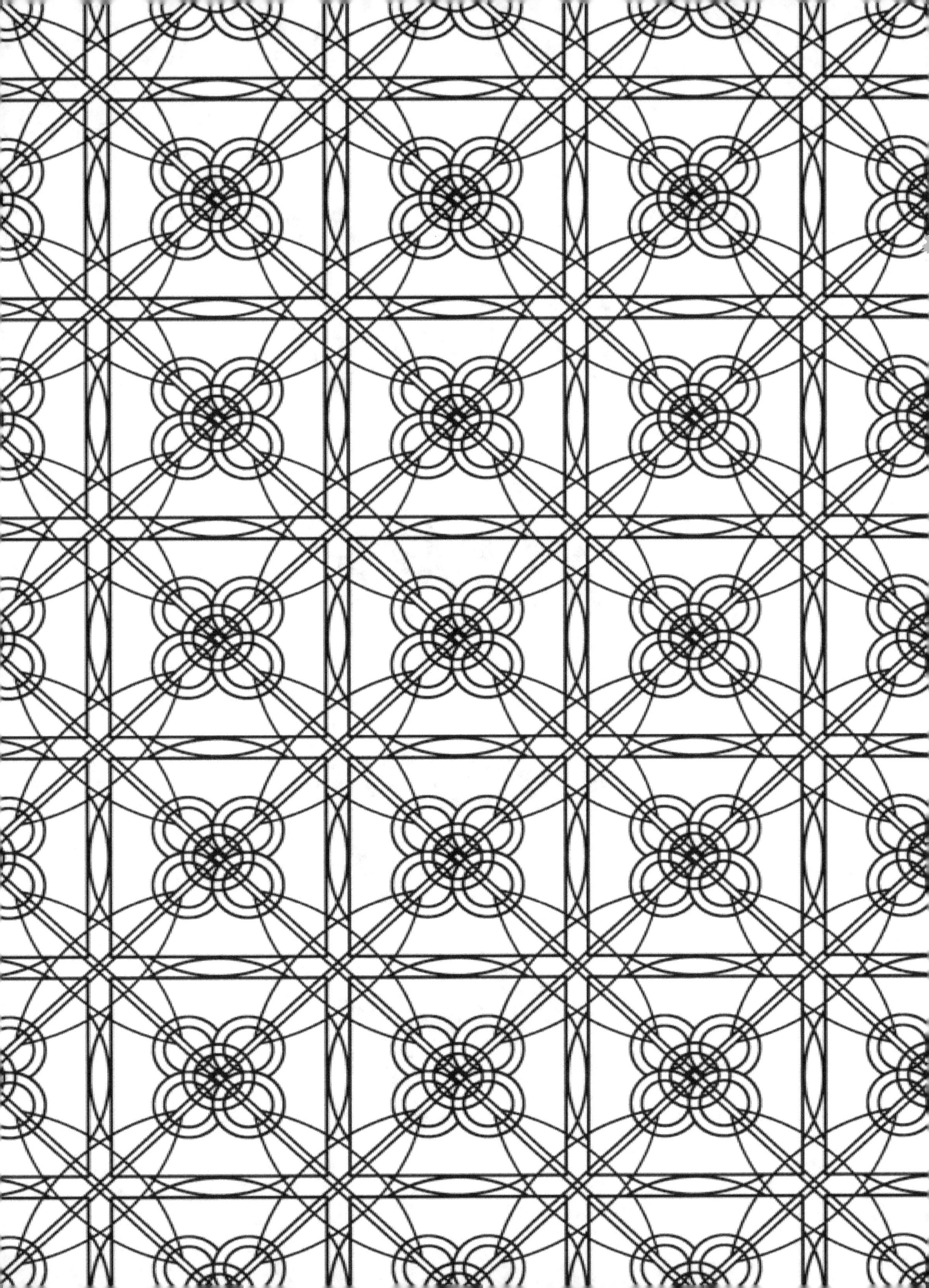

small steps every day

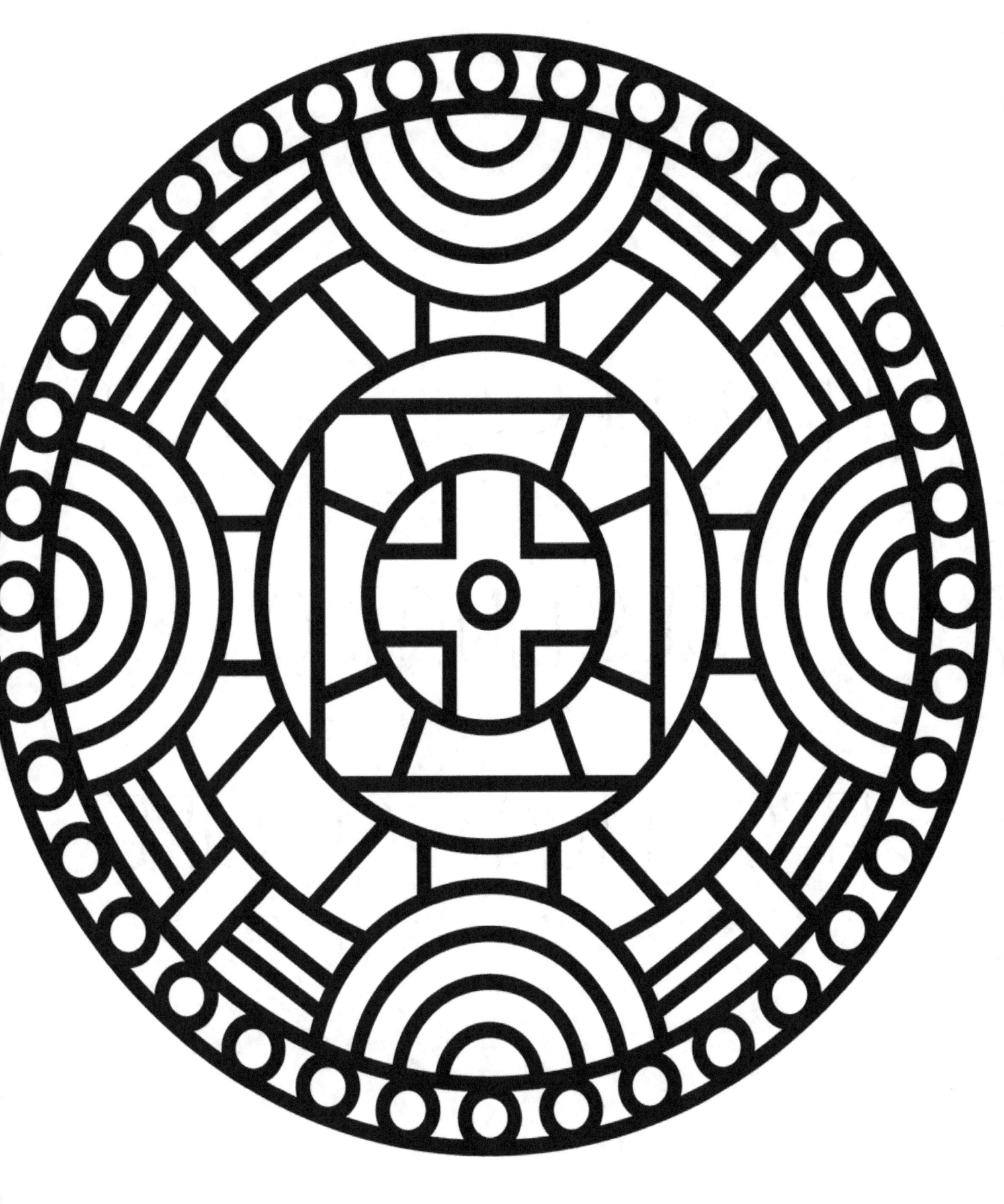

HAPPINESS IS NOT A

DESTINATION

IT'S A WAY OF LIFE

good

morning

sunshine

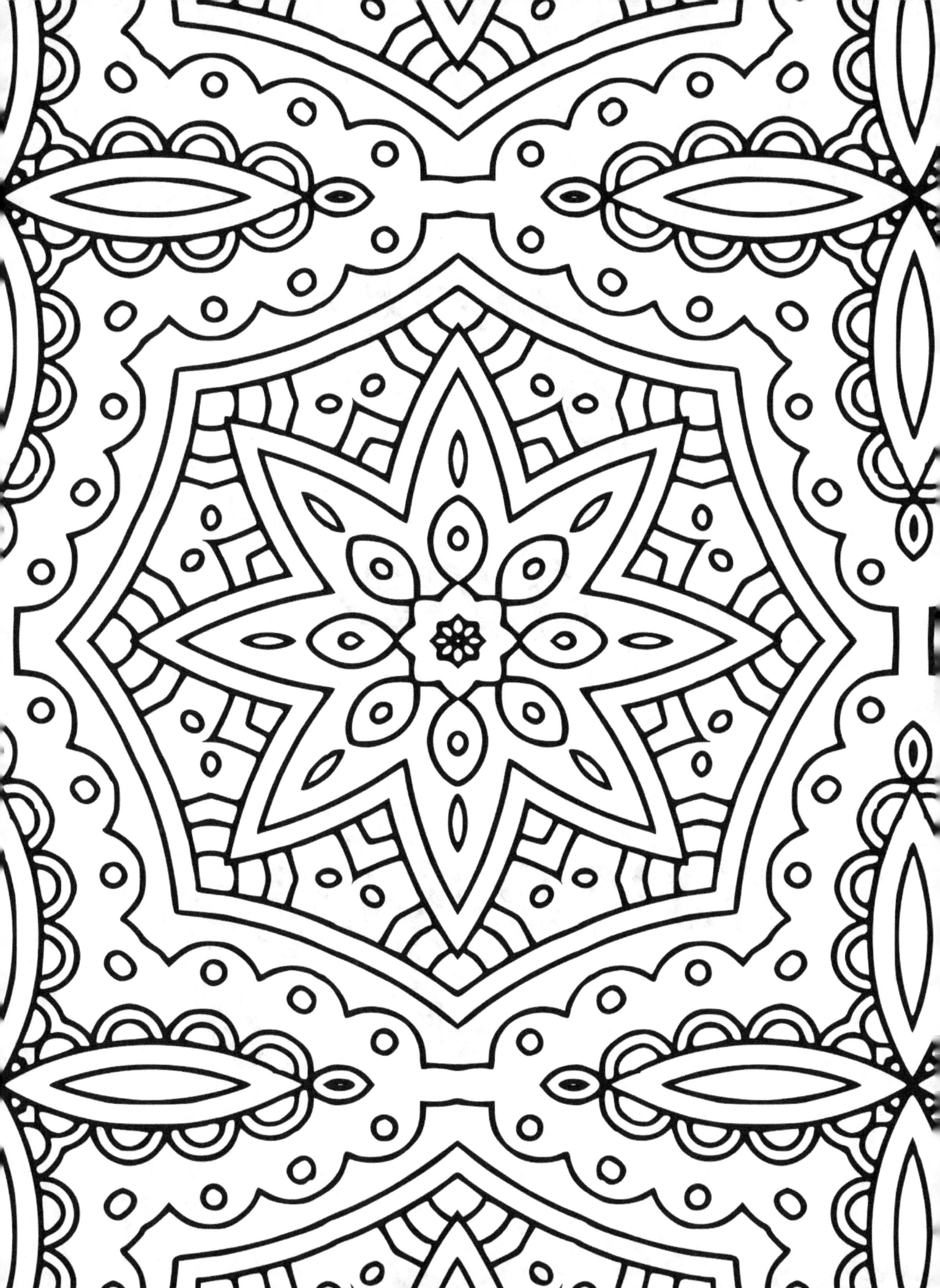

you are amazing

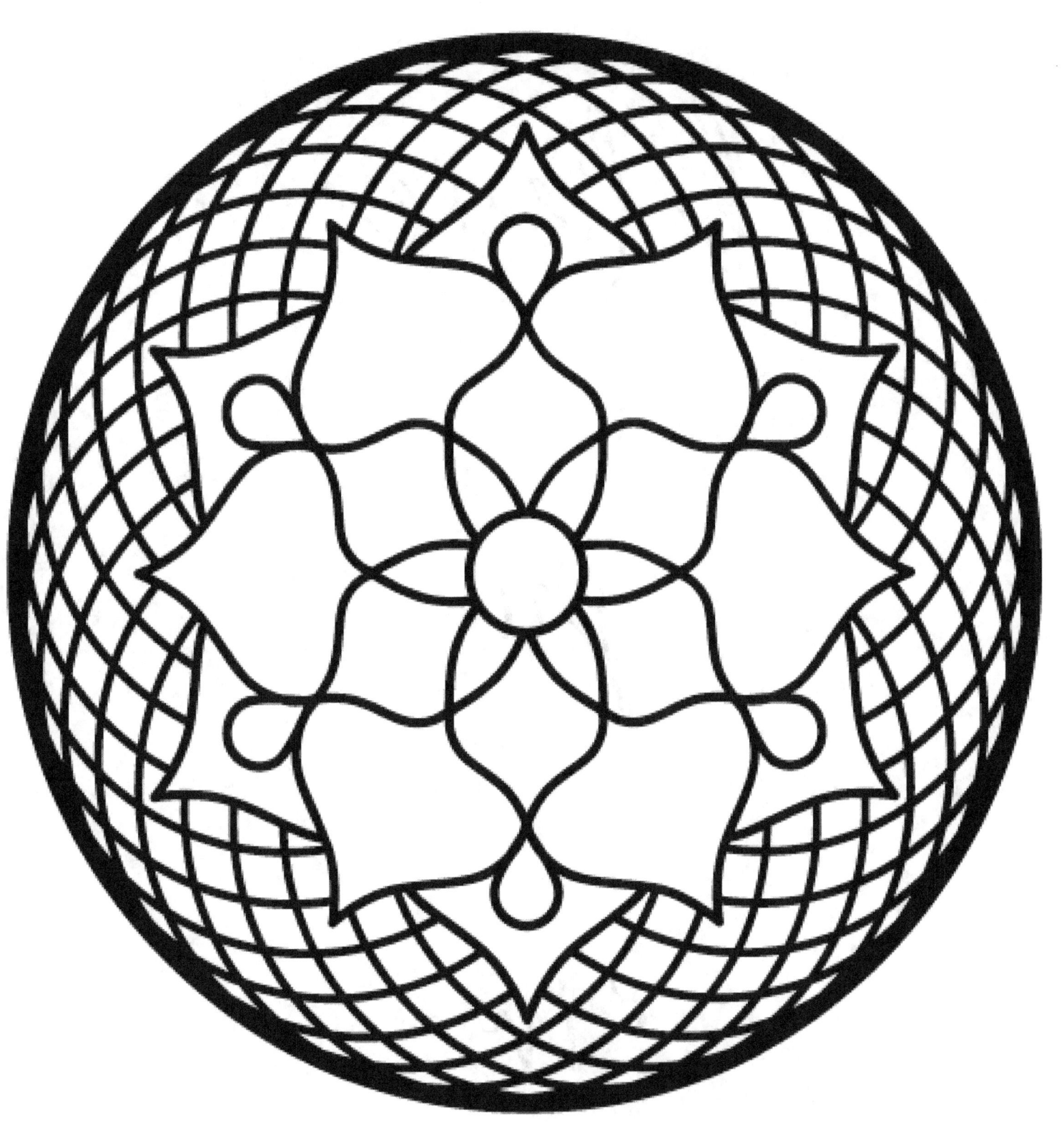

believe

you

can

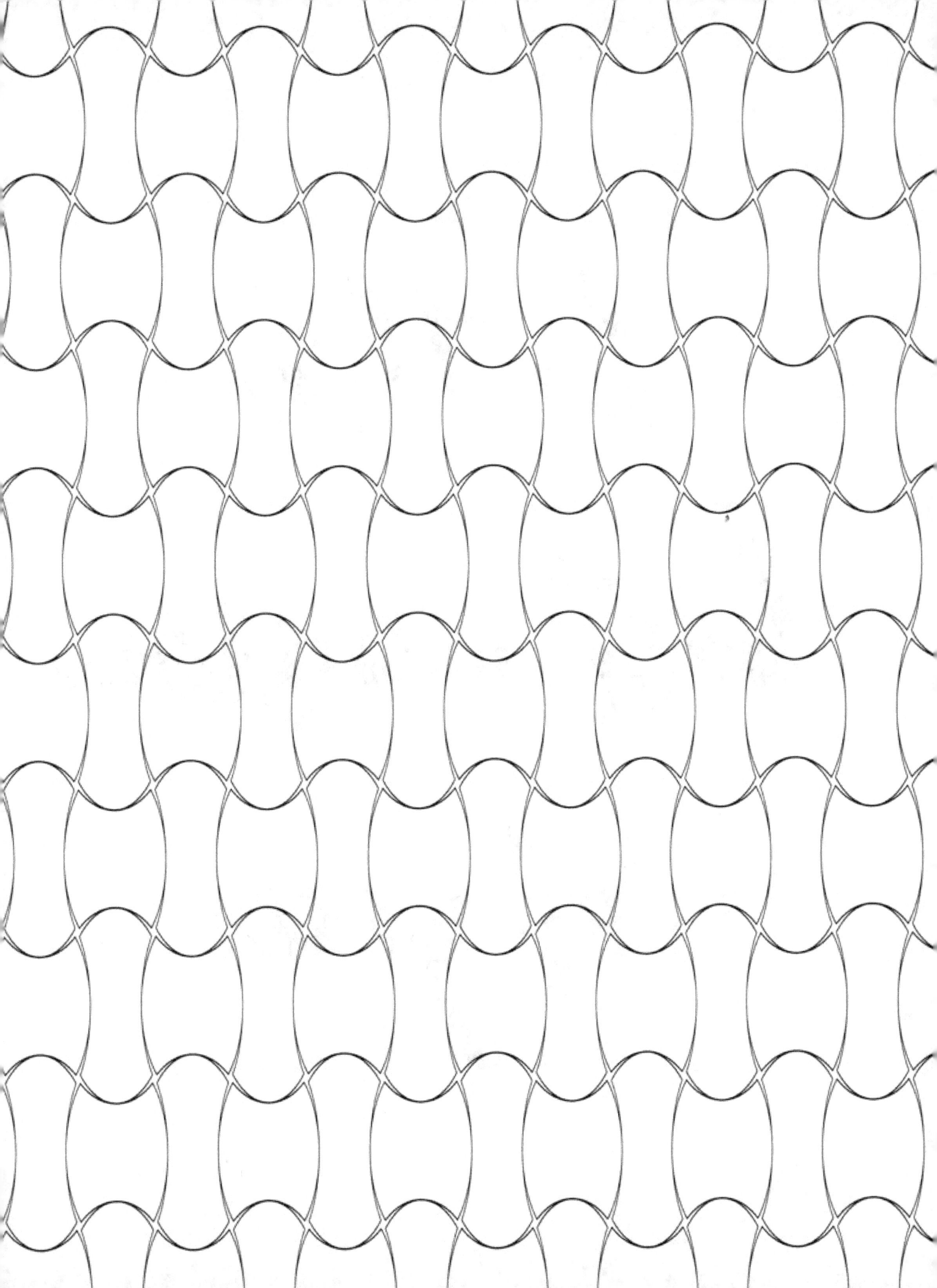

be the best version of you

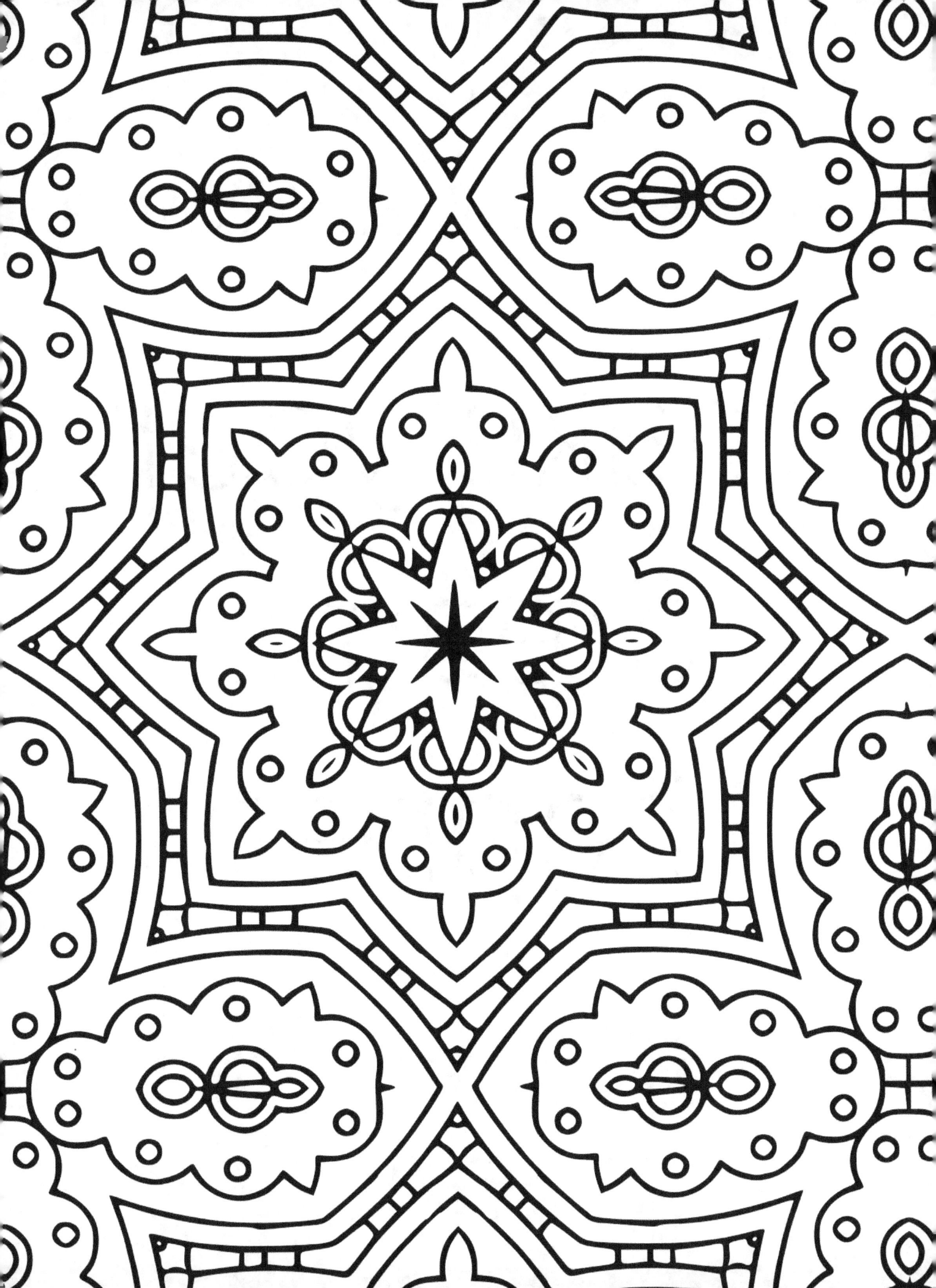

make your dreams happen

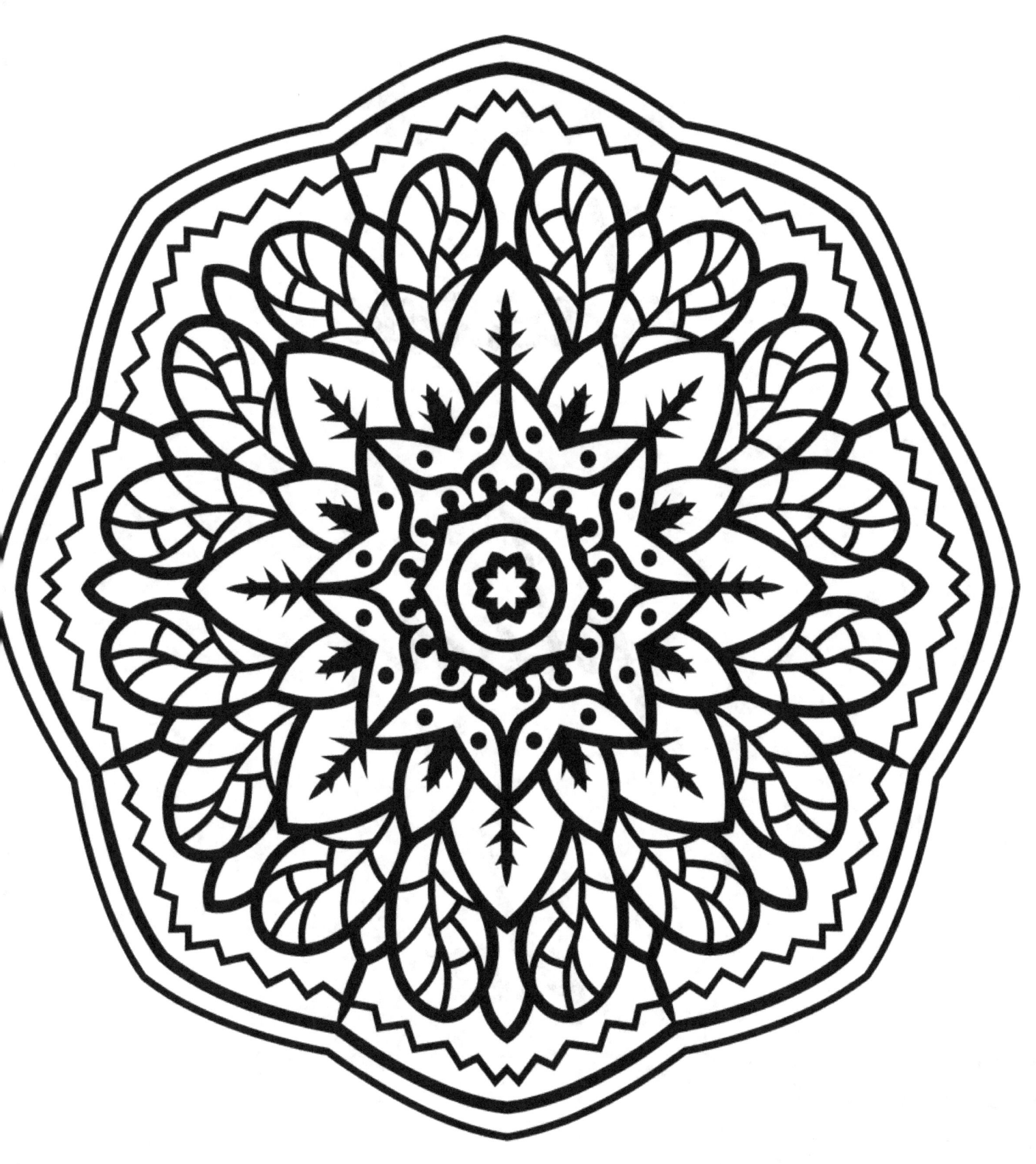

dream

plan

do

follow

your

heart

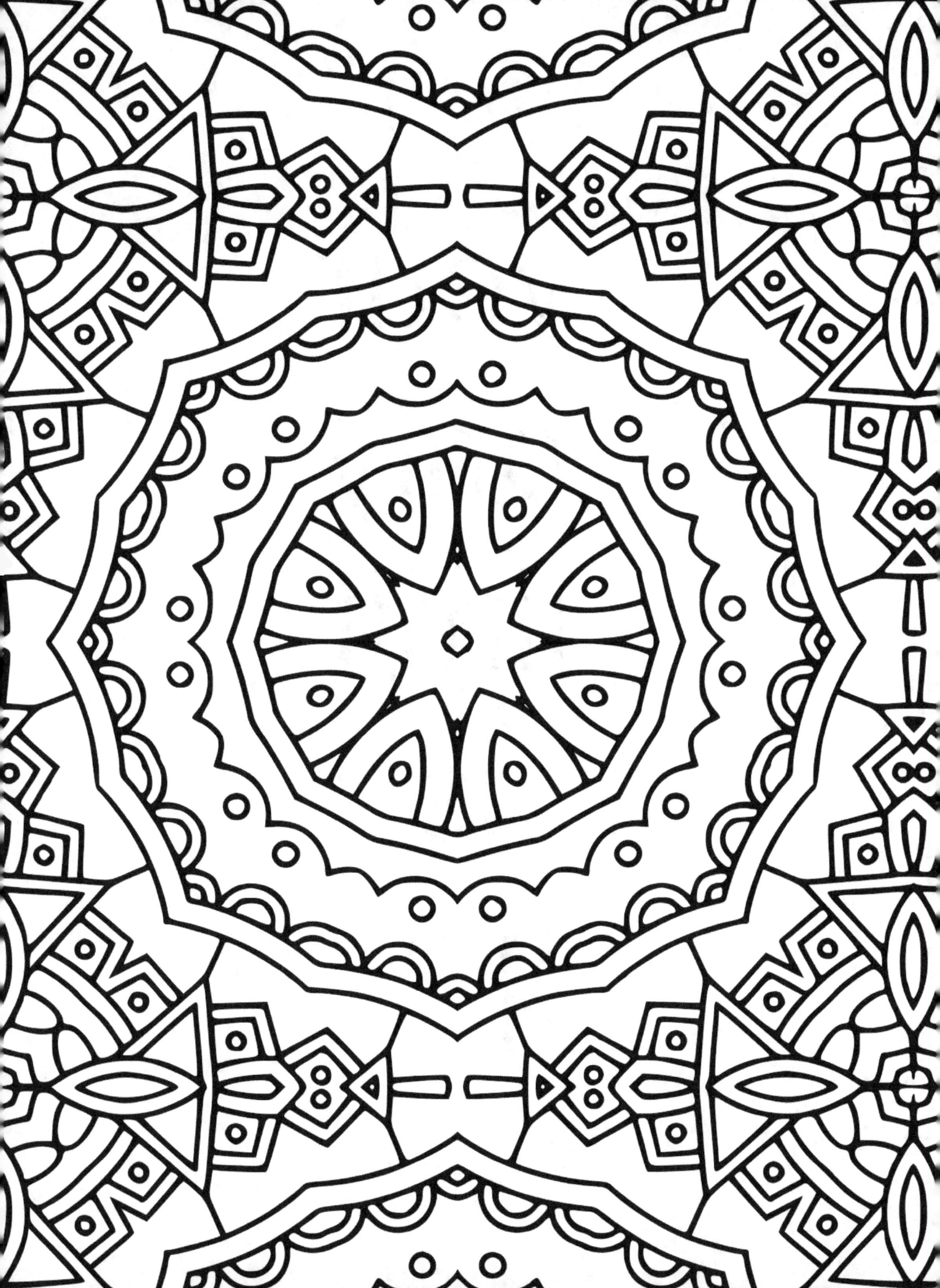

your
only
limit
is
you

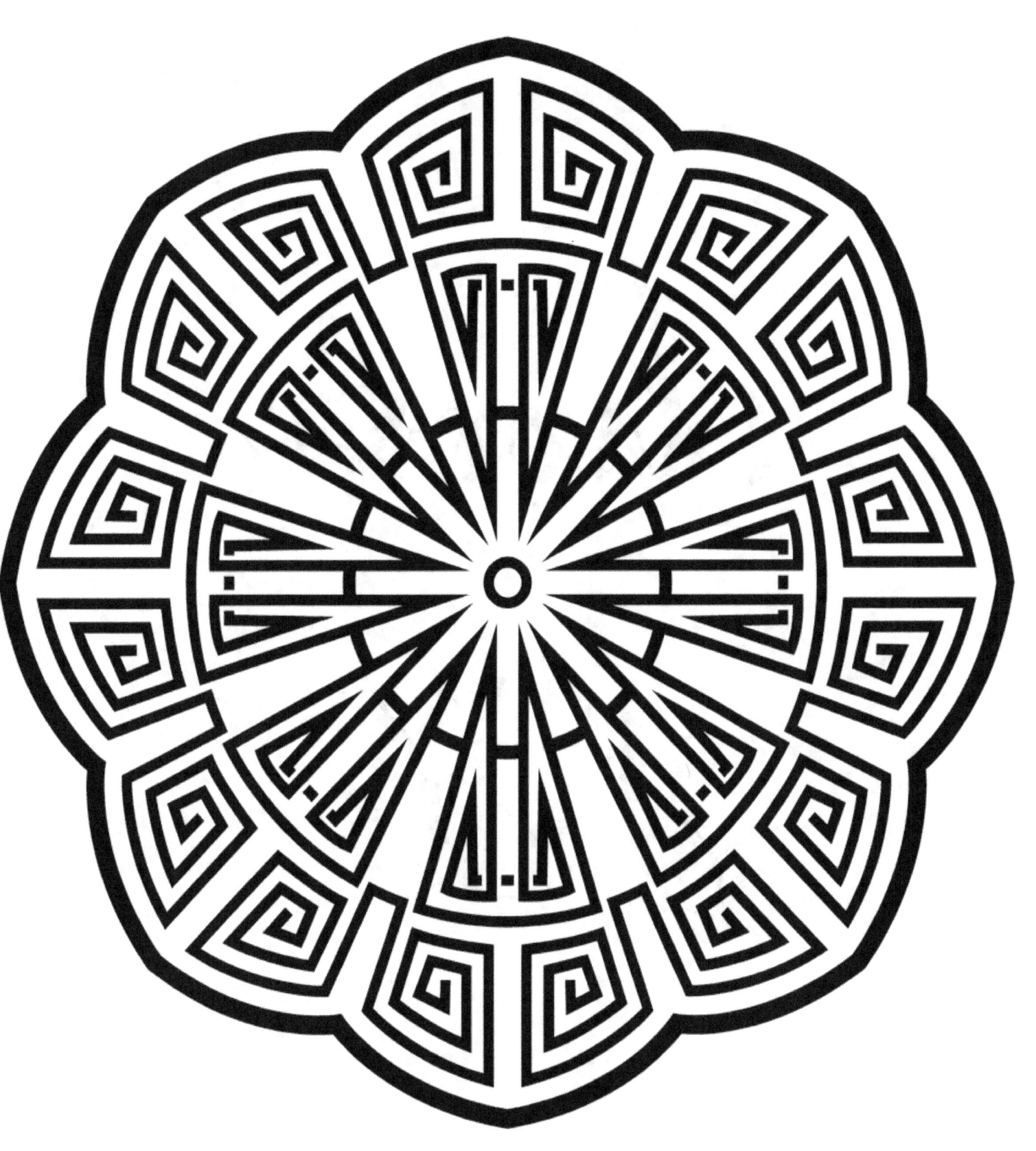

choose joy

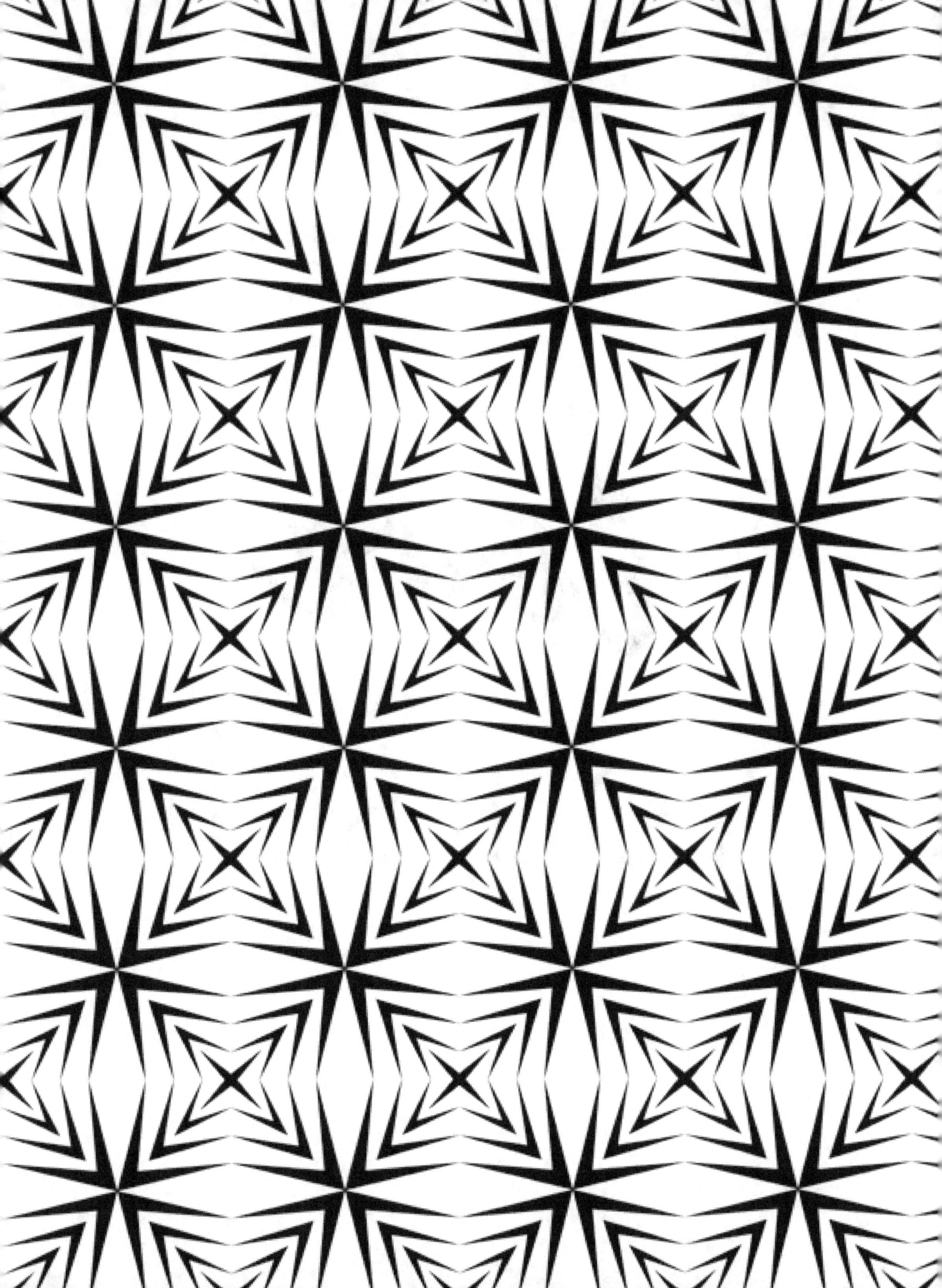

love
yourself

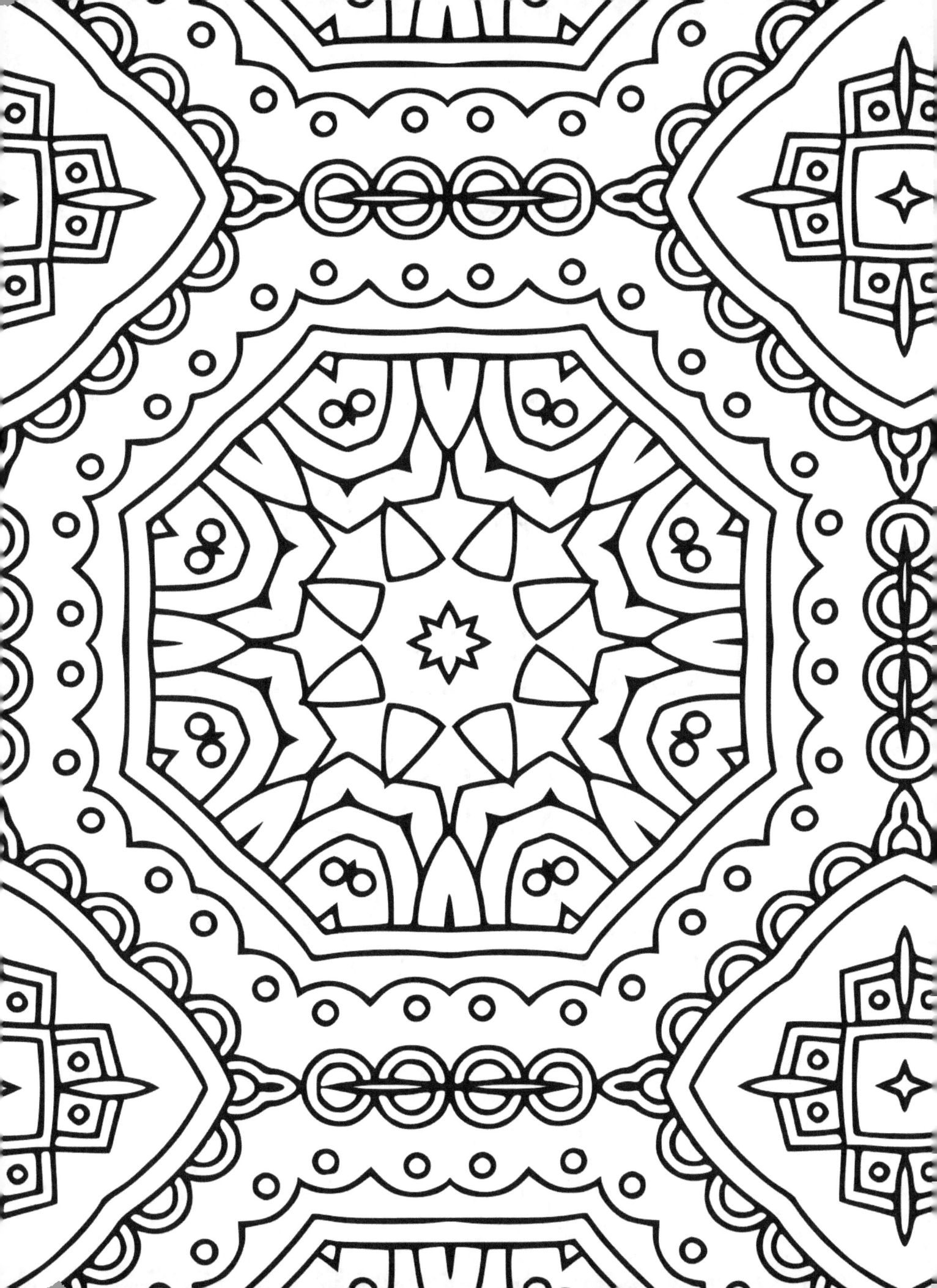

DON'T
LOOK BACK
YOU'RE NOT
GOING
THAT WAY

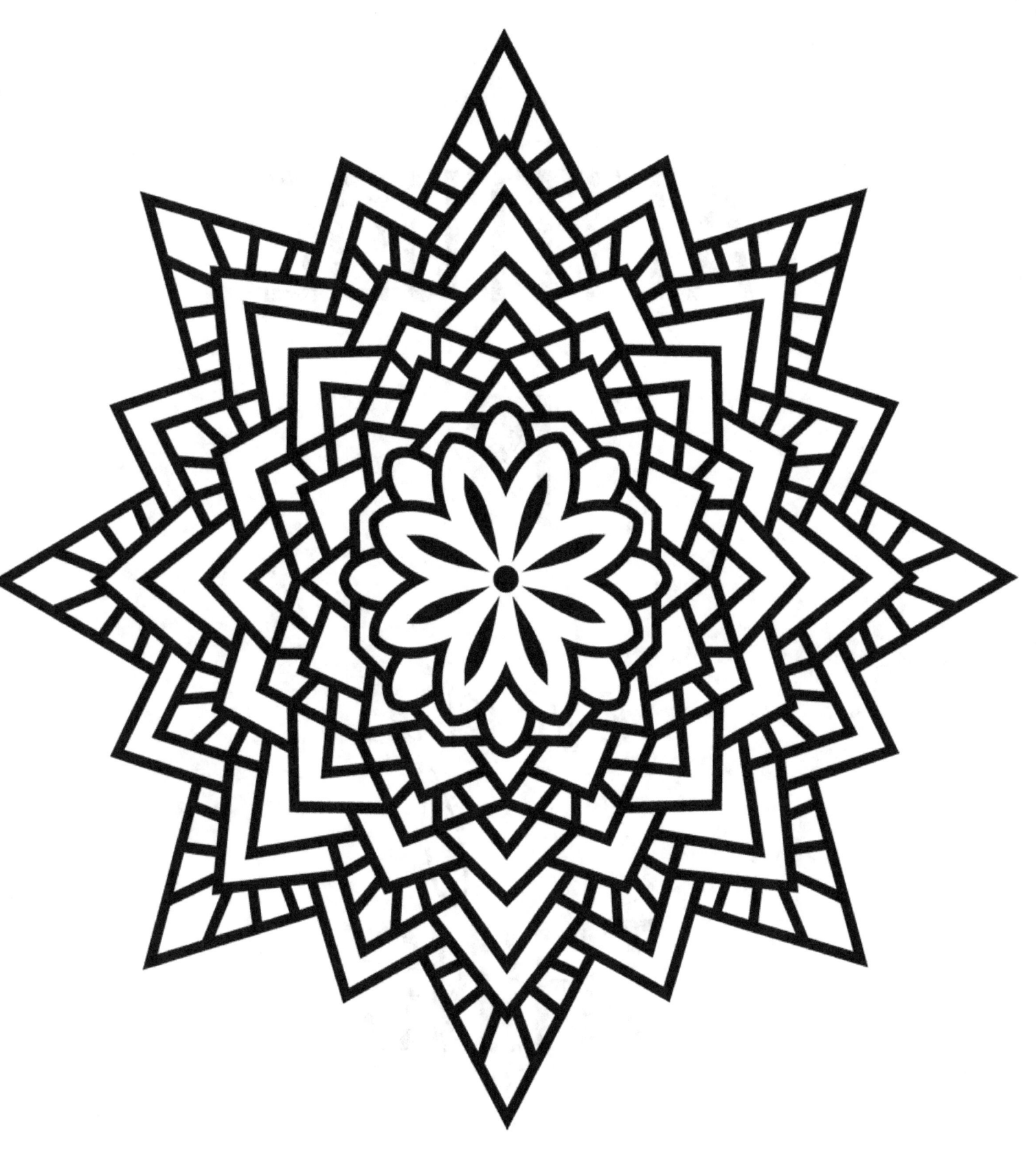

ATTITUDE IS *every* THING

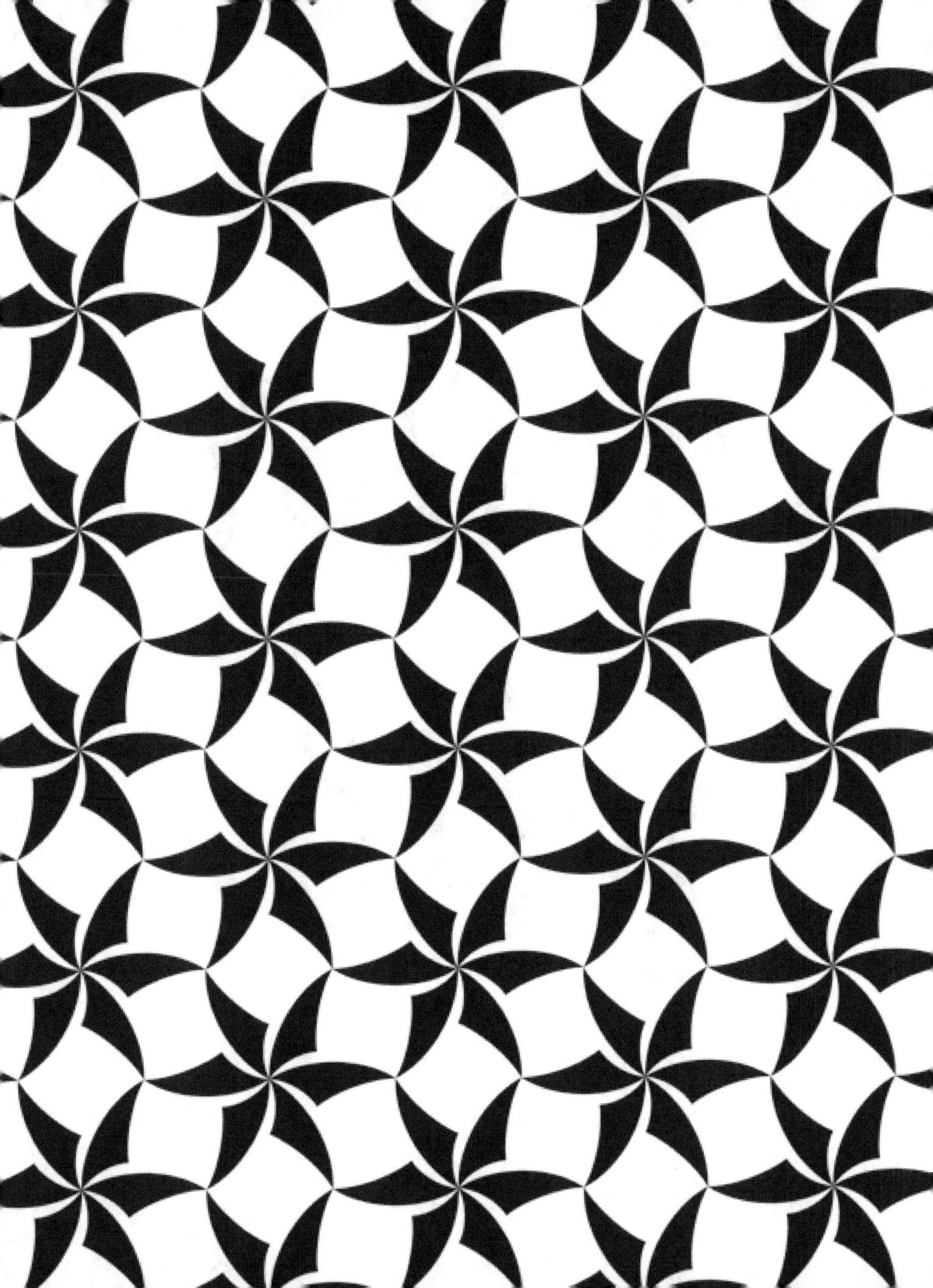

never settle

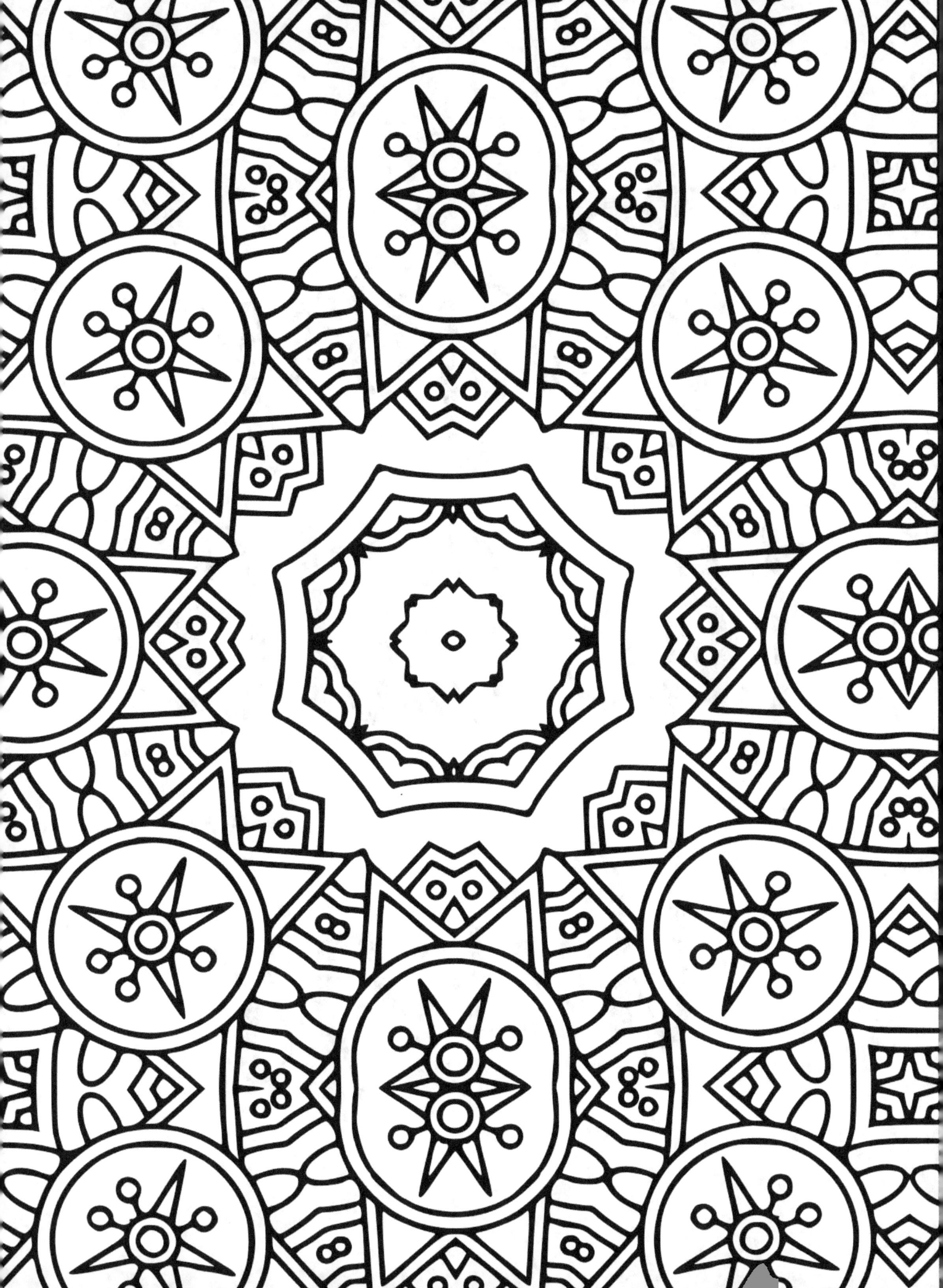

Enjoy the little things

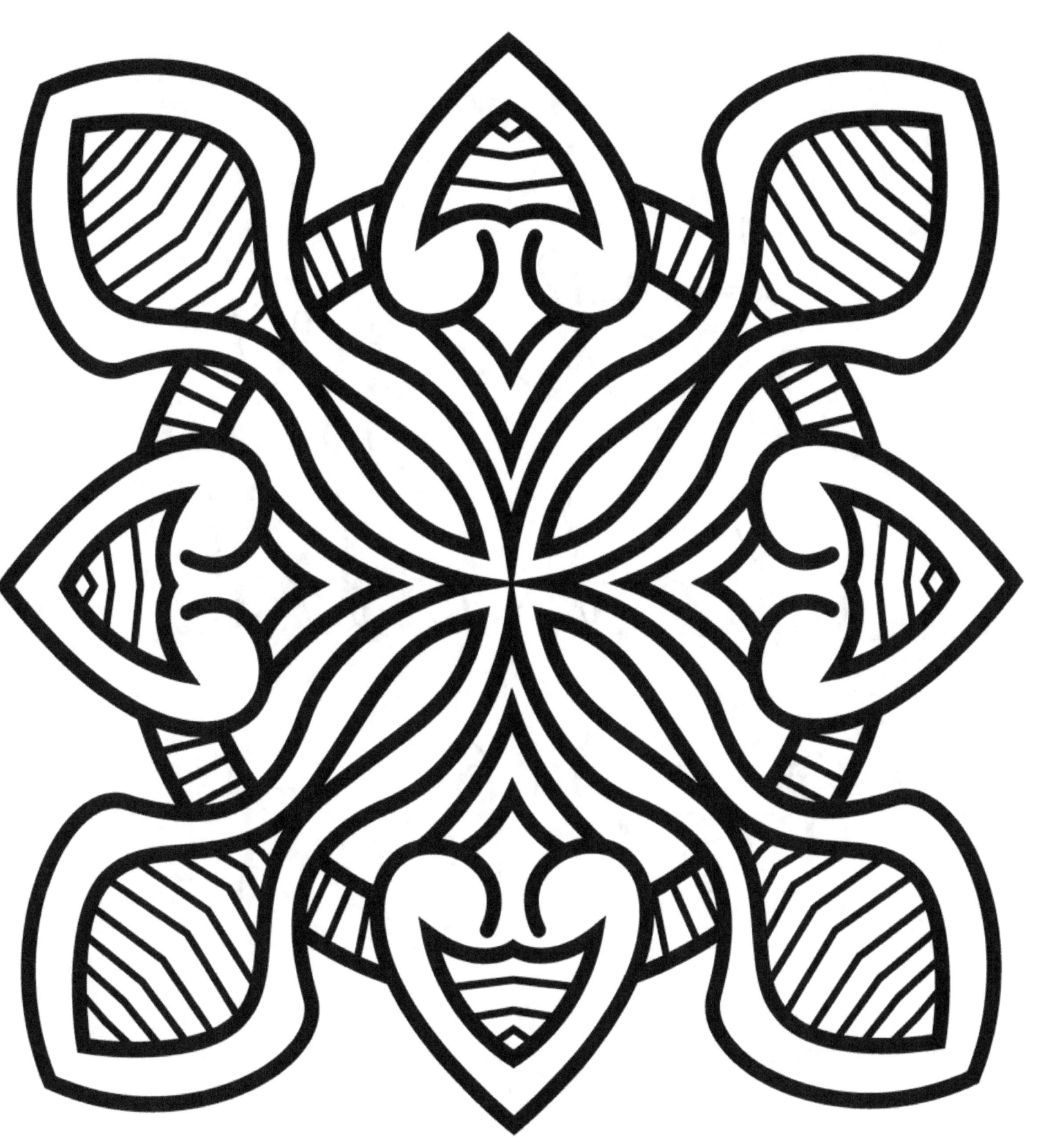

be the girl
who decided
to go for it.

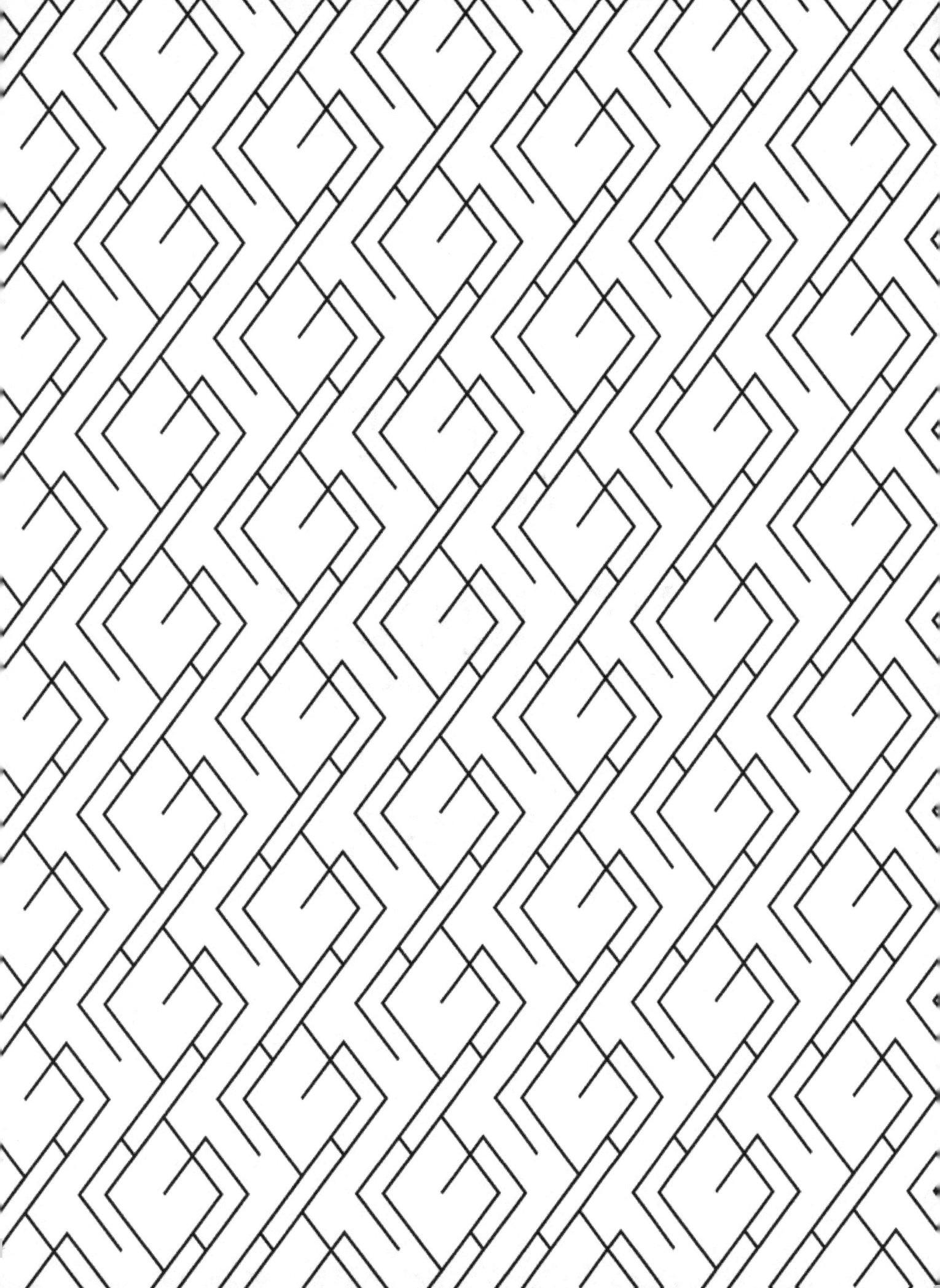

MAKE YOURSELF *proud*

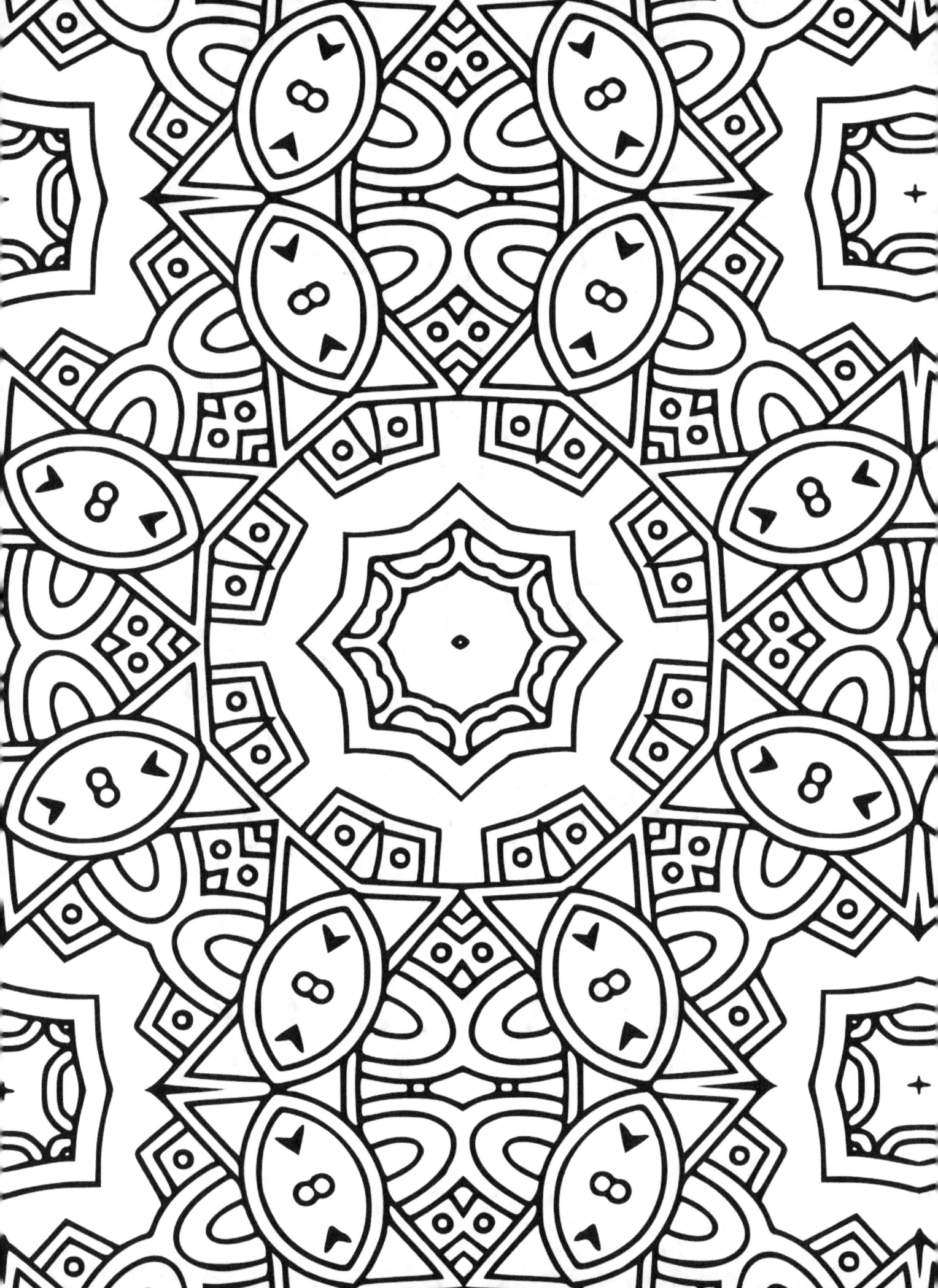

do good things and good things will come your way

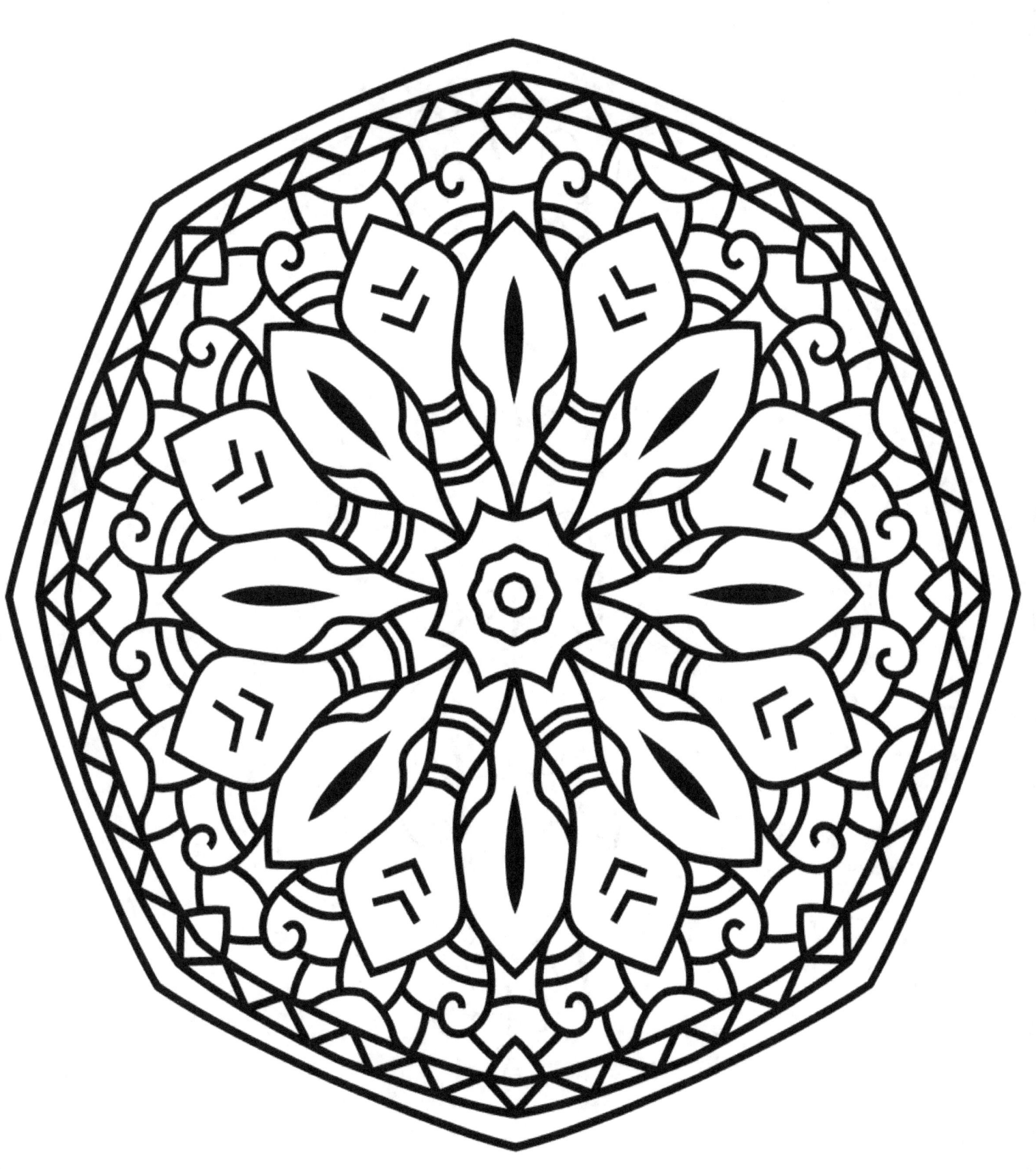

fall

in

love

with

life

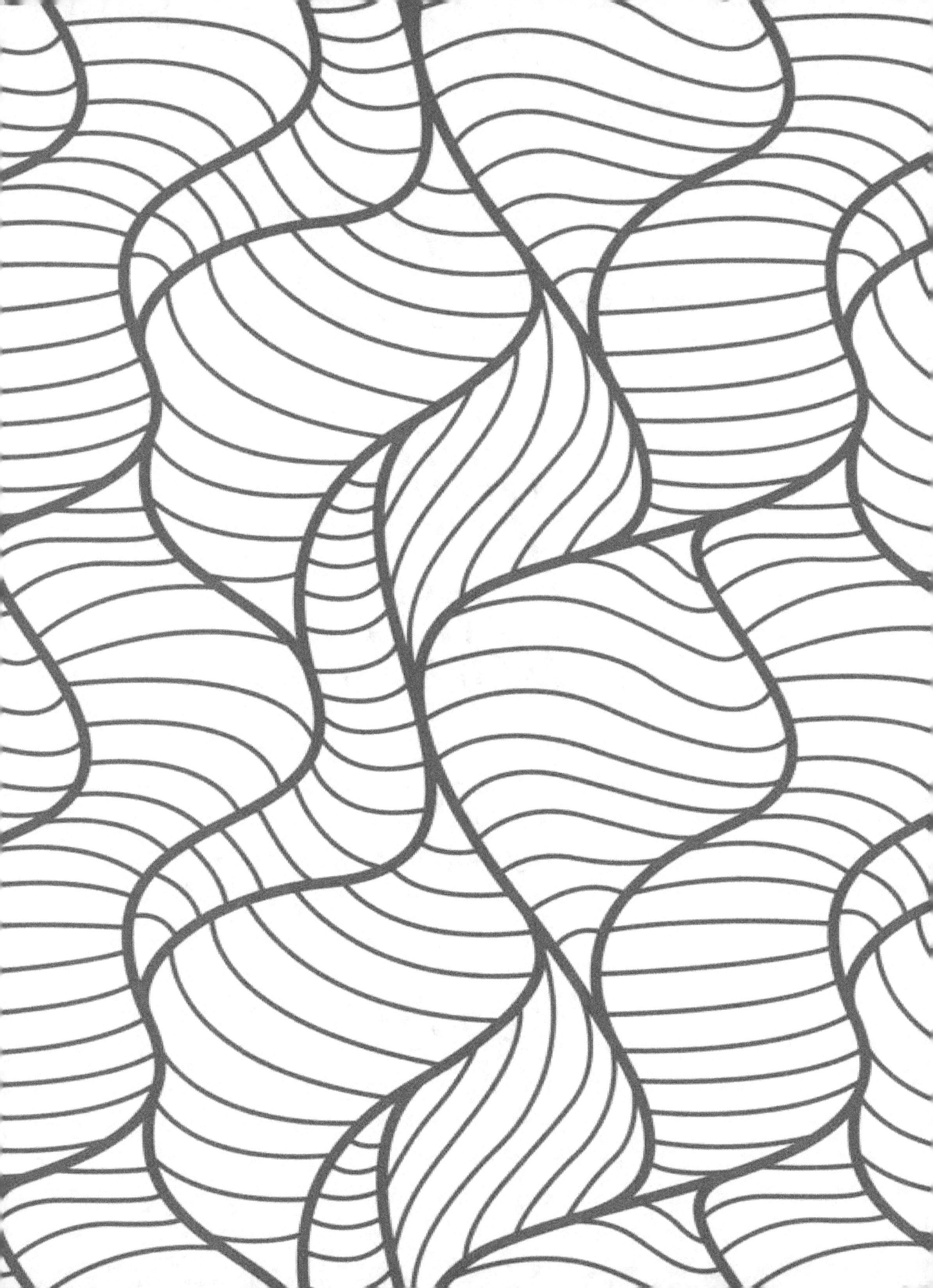

everything gets better with coffee

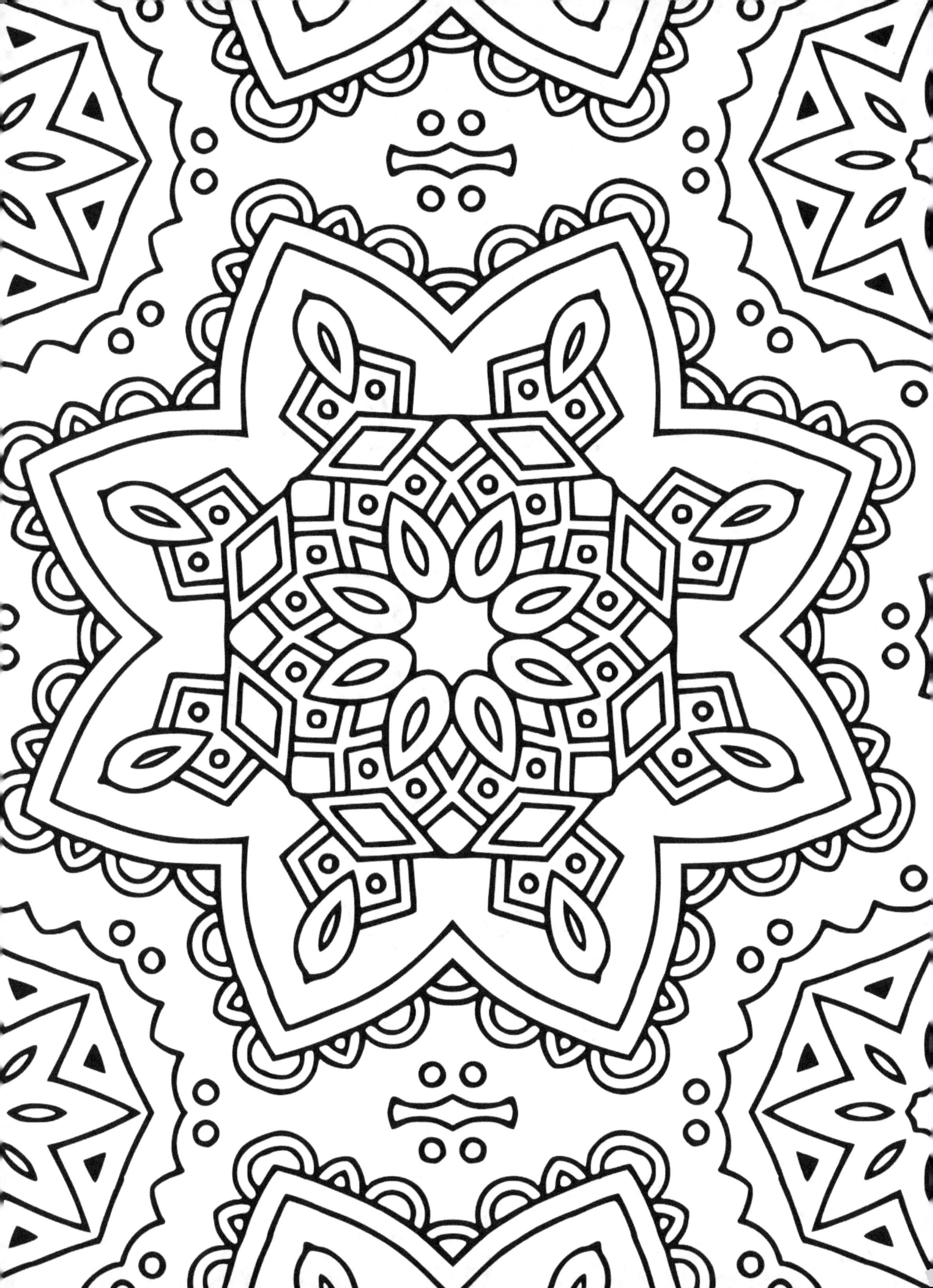

spread love everywhere you go

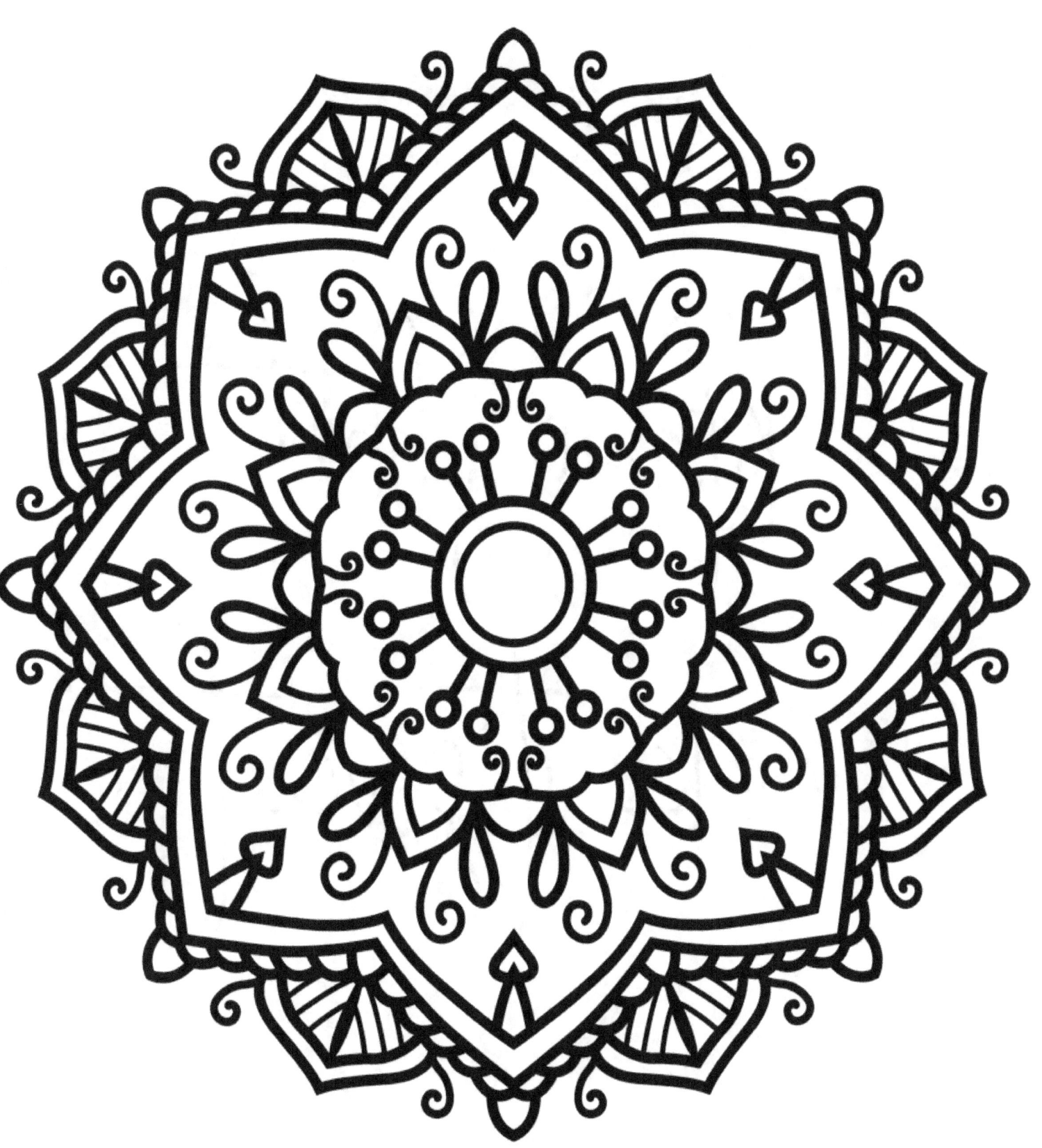

life is short

make it sweet

we

are

family

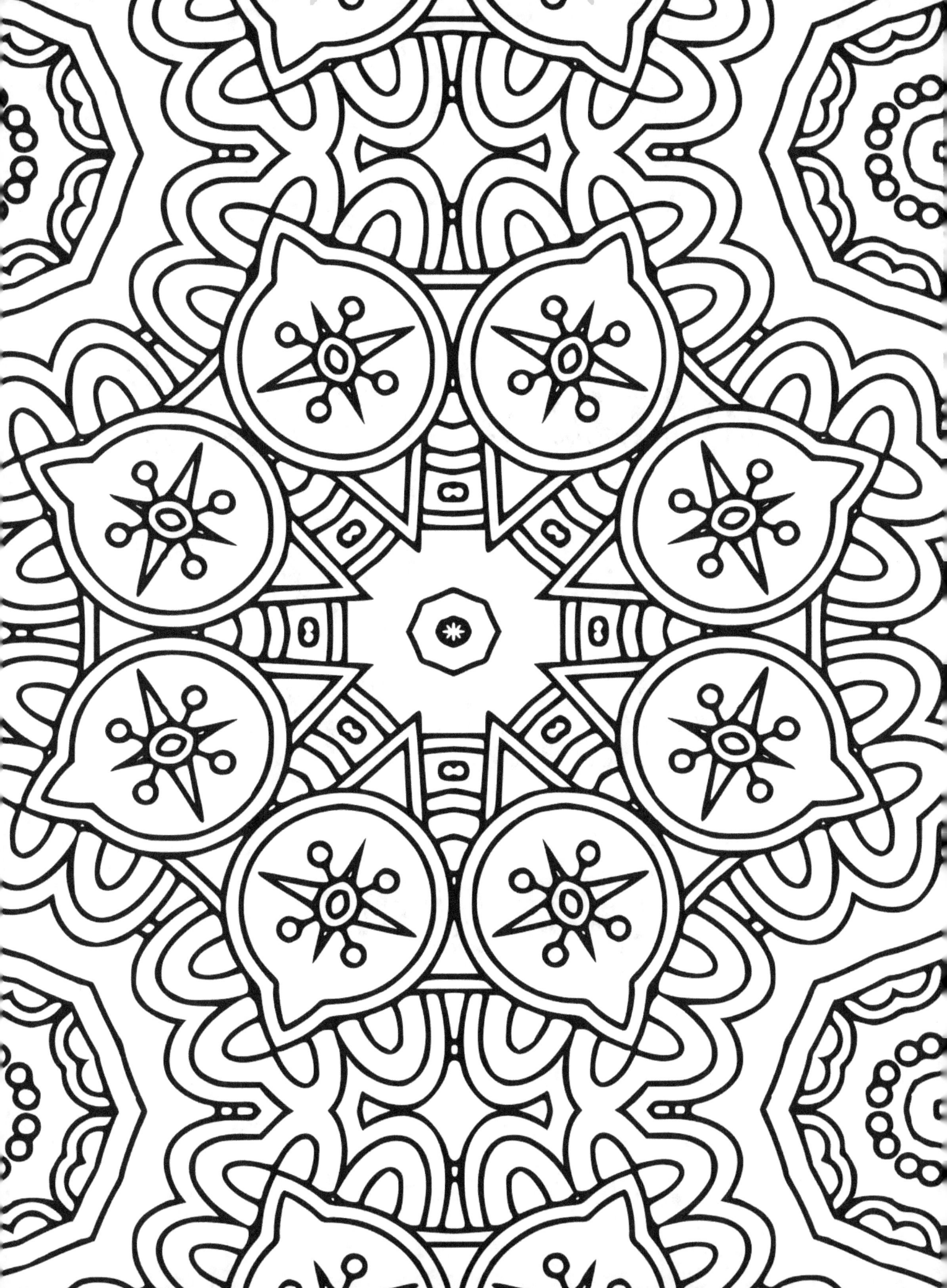

surround yourself with people who will help you grow.

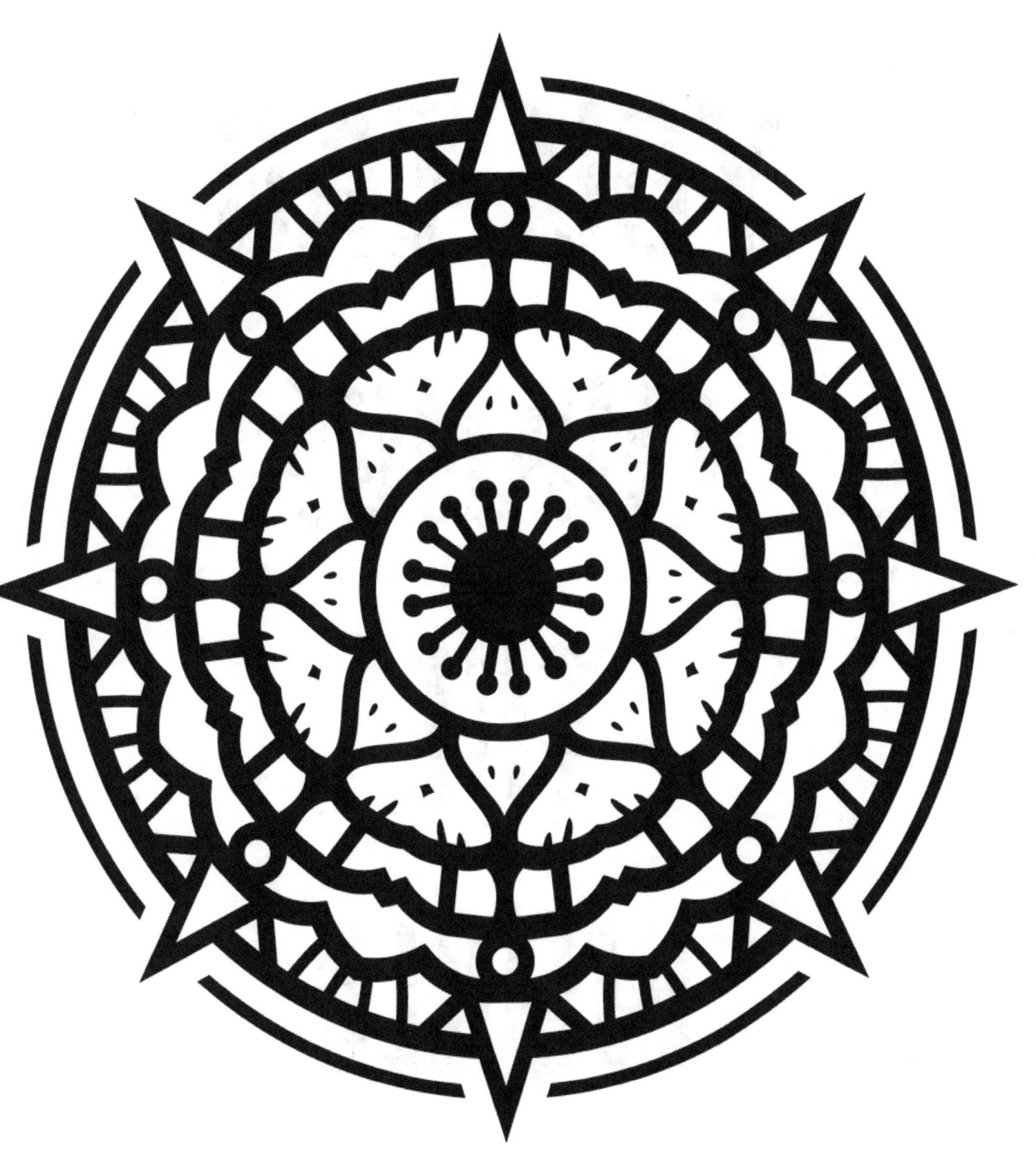

YOU CAN CHANGE THE WORLD

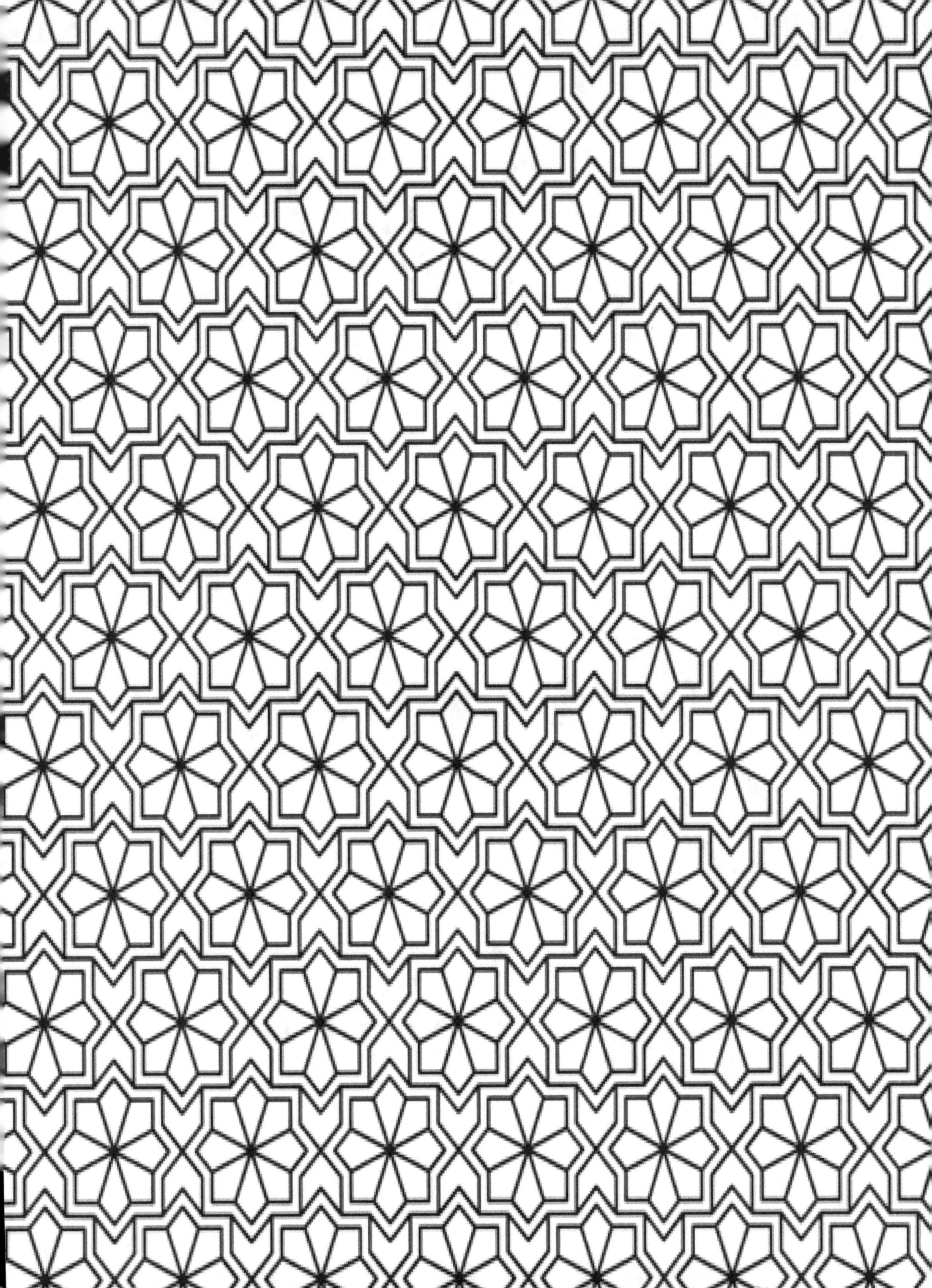

All you need is love

paint is temporary

quitting lasts forever

www.ingramcontent.com/pod-product-compliance
Lightning Source LLC
Chambersburg PA
CBHW080508220526
45465CB00006B/2409